MW00472854

THE
BOOK ON
MAKING MONEY

CHAPTER 1

PERSPECTIVES

My palms were sweating. I was about to march into my boss's office and ask him to triple my salary.

Who does this? This is crazy, said a voice in the back of my mind. It's a voice most people are familiar with, and one I often struggle to ignore.

It's the voice that wants you to stay in your comfort zone. It can be a useful tool to keep you out of trouble and stop you from doing stupid things. It can also hold you back from achieving success.

I decided I wasn't going to listen to it this time. I was going to walk down that hallway and demand a raise.

Any minute now.

I sat at my desk, staring at a cold cup of coffee and my laptop, which had gone into sleep mode twenty minutes ago.

Be grateful for what you have, the voice said.

I was. Two years before, I'd been sitting in a filing room for a few bucks an hour. I'd spent a long time unemployed before landing this job eight months ago. The country was in the middle of a recession, and I was grateful to have a job, but I had a promise to keep.

I stood up, resolved to march down the hallway. After all, what was the worst that could happen?

The armchair.

The memory of the comfy light-blue chair flying out of my boss's office and bouncing down the hallway flashed in my brain. I could still hear the string of profanities that followed it.

Do you really want to have an armchair thrown at you?

I'd been at this job for less than a year, and I'd already seen Brad, my boss, make several people cry. The company was a start-up with hundreds of millions of dollars in investment capital, and they'd managed to blow through it in record time. It was high stakes and high energy, and exactly where I wanted to be.

You're already in over your head.

It's true. I was managing a massive, eight-figure marketing budget. Before this job the most I'd ever been responsible for was a few hundred dollars at a time. I hadn't slept more than five hours a night since I'd started working for Brad. My coffee consumption was reaching dangerous levels.

You haven't even been here twelve months. Don't you normally bring this stuff up at your annual review?

It was a strange thought. I don't think anyone normally asks for a 200 percent raise during their annual review.

Is this really the right time?

The company had just gone through a restructuring, and a lot of people at the top, including Brad, had taken pay cuts. The housing bubble had burst the year before. The economy was in shambles.

Would he fire me for asking for a raise? Would I look really greedy?

The voice was working overtime.

You're going to get fired. You won't be able to support your family. You don't have a college degree. You won't be able to get another office job. You'll have to go back to working a register at McDonald's.

Just stay at your desk.

I took a swig of cold coffee, drew a deep breath, and collected myself. The voice had run out of objections and was finally silent.

I stood up, tucked in my shirt, and walked down the hallway to Brad's office.

"Can I talk to you for a minute?"

Brad nodded, putting his phone down.

I closed the door behind me, hoping he didn't see my hand shaking.

Then I asked him for a $150,000 raise.

YOU WANT TO LEARN HOW TO MAKE MONEY

If you've tried to find answers to your questions about money, you've probably run into two very different approaches to the subject.

The first way people will tell you to build wealth is one that we hear all the time, whether we want to or not. How many times have you seen ads like these on the internet?

MAKE MONEY WHILE YOU SLEEP!
MAKE MILLIONS ON eBAY/AMAZON!
MAKE SIX FIGURES WORKING AN HOUR A DAY!

Though most of us know these ads are scams, there are sadly some people who fall for them. Often the people selling these dreams of wealth didn't have any money until they convinced others to pay them for financial advice. Many of these scammers are just recruiting other people to do their work for them. You do all the work, and they keep most of the money.

You'll never get rich that way.

These programs are designed to prey on people's desire to get rich quick with very little effort.

The truth is, there are legitimate ways to do all of those things (make money in your sleep, work an hour a day), and yes, I'll go more into that later. In the meantime, stay away from these programs.

If you're serious about being wealthy, this is probably not the first book you've read on how to become rich. You're probably already familiar with the other approach to becoming wealthy, the one I call: *GET RICH VERY, VERY, VERY SLOWLY.*

You might recognize some of this advice:

Cut back on expenses
Pay off your debt
Save $10 (or $50, or $100) every month
Open a 401(k)
Invest in real estate, mutual funds, etc.

This is all very sound advice.

Unfortunately, it won't make you rich—at least not anytime soon. It always involves some form of living beneath your means while you save for retirement. A lot of these books have charts showing you how much you need to save each month so you can be a millionaire forty or fifty years from now.

There are plenty of these books out there. If your idea of being rich just means gaining more financial security by cutting back on your expenses, I suggest you read one of them instead. They're full of great advice for the average person.

"It's not sexy," they'll tell you about their advice on saving money, but it's well worth it when you finally have that nest egg.

They're right. It's not sexy. I don't know about you, but I wouldn't want to wait forty years to be wealthy.

I read several books about getting rich back when I couldn't afford to pay rent, and every one infuriated me. They were all useless in my situation.

The reason the strategies those books promote won't make you rich anytime soon is found in their central message: cut back, get out of debt, then make your money work for you.
Save and invest. The more you save, the more you invest, the harder your money works.

Well, I had no debt. I also had no money. As someone who had no money, I can tell you this: money can't work for you if you don't have any.

Saving is very important, but most investment strategies are just ways for wealthy people to get wealthier. If you invest $100, you'd be really lucky if you got $10 a year in return. If you invest $10 million at the same rate, you get a million dollars a year in return.

The thing is, rich people don't need a book on how to get rich. Just like poor people don't need a book to tell them how to make their money work for them.

They need someone to tell them how to make money.

I didn't want someone to tell me how to make $10 by investing $100. I wanted someone to tell me how to get $10 million so I could live off a million dollars a year in interest.

This book is not for rich people trying to get richer, and it's not for middle-class or poor people who want to live with less so that, one day, just before they die, they can say that they are wealthy on paper, even though they never got to enjoy their wealth.

If average isn't good enough for you, if your idea of being rich means a better lifestyle than the one you're currently living, and if you want to build wealth while you still have plenty of life left to enjoy it, then this book is for you.

CHANGE YOUR PERSPECTIVE

The purpose of this book is to change your perspective on money.

It doesn't teach you how to create a pyramid scheme to take money from your friends and relatives.

This book is not about filling out online surveys for cash.

It's not about multi-level marketing.

It's not about get-rich-quick schemes or get-rich-slow plans.

This book is designed to change the way you look at wealth. It will show you how blind adherence to certain misconceptions prevents most people from getting ahead. By reading this book, you'll get a clearer picture of how money really works, and realize the way you've been taught to think about money is all wrong.

Once your perspective on money changes, it's a lot easier to build wealth whether you own your own business or you work for someone else. I've had success with both paths, and I'll teach you ways to recreate that success for yourself.

WHY SHOULD YOU LISTEN TO ME?

What can someone who was *born* rich teach you about *becoming* rich?

They could probably tell you what it's like to be rich, but not much about how to go from a minimum-wage job to financial independence.

What can someone who had one great idea for a product that made him a fortune teach you about making money?

Hey, have a great idea, and you'll be rich.

Not too helpful.

That's why there's not a lot of good information out there on how to get rich. Some people who are extremely wealthy inherited their money. Many more achieved wealth with a lot of luck by taking risks. That's not to say it didn't take a lot of work or that they don't deserve their good fortune—they took the risk and deserve the reward—but we all know that working hard alone won't make you rich.

Unfortunately, the wealthy can't teach you how to be lucky.

So who can teach you how to be rich?

I don't have a doctorate in money management. I don't have a master's, bachelor's, or even an associate's degree in anything. To be honest, I barely graduated high school. When it comes time to talk to my kids about the importance of getting good grades in school, their mother will have to handle that conversation.

Why would you take advice from a guy who spent years never making much more than minimum wage, bouncing between jobs at McDonald's, Taco Bell, and the local movie theater?

As it turns out, there's a very good reason.

I'd always known what you were "supposed" to do to make money—go to school to get a job that pays well, or well enough. Work at that job for fifty years and then, if you're still alive, retire and enjoy your last few years on earth.

That sounded like the worst idea in the world.

In fact, my teenage brain couldn't think of anything more terrifying.

So, in typical teenage fashion, I made up my mind:

I'll show them.

So I didn't go to college. I didn't get a job that paid well. I was always late on my rent, until finally I couldn't afford a place of my own and had to couch surf. I didn't know how to make money, and there was no one to teach me. My parents had no money. They spent a large part of my childhood in crushing debt and working low-wage jobs.

I wasn't doing any better. For a while I lived on as little as $2 a day for food. I'd walk to the grocery store and come back with 39-cent burritos and ramen packets.

If I was going to treat myself, I'd get a $1 double cheeseburger from the Hardee's up the road.

Some college students will understand the lifestyle, but this wasn't college. I was a poor working adult. This was my life, and I saw no way out.

I thought I was a smart guy, but somehow I was the poorest person I knew.

Why am I telling you all this?

I want you to know that not every story about wealth is just about some guy getting lucky. It's easy to assume everyone who's made a lot of money had advantages you'll never have. Then you can shrug your shoulders and believe success simply isn't meant for you. You can listen to that voice in your head that stops you from doing anything scary.

You'd be rich, too, if you had those advantages, it says.

I used to think that way. If I were luckier, I'd be rich. If my parents were wealthy, I'd be on easy street. If I were smarter, I could come up with a brilliant invention and make boatloads of cash.

I had none of those advantages.

So why listen to someone like me?

Here's why:

I didn't build my wealth on the back of an inheritance.

My parents couldn't bail me out when I got into money trouble.

I didn't come up with a brilliant idea that changed an industry and made me billions.

I didn't invent something really cool that everyone had to have.

I didn't win the lottery.

I didn't make a ton of money by betting on stocks.

I don't have a college degree.

If grades are any indication, I'm not the smartest man in the room.

Yet I was still able to achieve financial success at a young age.

You should listen to me because chances are you're already ahead of where I was when I started (and if you're not, don't worry). If I could become a millionaire in a few years just by changing the way I thought about money, then the odds are even better for you.

You should listen to me because if I could do it, you can do it, too.

IS IT REPRODUCIBLE?

There's one more reason why you should listen to me.

Imagine if a clone of Bill Gates, one of the richest men in America, was created today and grew up in a middle-class household.

Bill Jr. would be very smart. He'd probably be great with computers.

But would Bill Jr. become a billionaire?

Maybe, but the odds would be very strongly against him.

Getting rich from good ideas and creating new industries is very dependent on being at the right place at the right time. It requires skill and hard work, but so many brilliant and hard-working men and women have failed because the timing was less than perfect.

On the other hand, someone who learns how to make money can create wealth regardless of the time and place she lives in.

If you learn how to make money, you don't need to have groundbreaking ideas to be successful. You don't need to be the next Bill Gates or Steve Jobs. If you learn how to make money, you can be successful in the industry of your choice. You can do the things you want to do and get paid for it.

WHAT'S YOUR CURRENT PERSPECTIVE?

When you grow up in a religious household on the low end of the income spectrum, it's easy to come away with the idea that money is evil.

In fact, the Bible even says, "For the love of money is the root of all kinds of evil."

There's a stigma that many of us attach to even talking about money, unless it's about how little of it you have. Sometimes it seems like there's a badge of honor associated with getting by on next to nothing. Whoever is suffering more is the winner.

I had the impression that the poor could enjoy life better than the wealthy. They could appreciate the small things—when you don't have much, you're grateful for what you have.

The rich, by contrast, must all be miserable. Sure, they had their cars and mansions and yachts, but were they really happy?

I'm convinced this is why we love tabloids so much. We need to know that the lives of these rich, successful people are totally, utterly miserable. It gives us

11

a sense of justice knowing that karma is keeping things equal. We can be smug in poverty, because we must be getting ahead in other, less tangible areas. Besides, they probably cheated to get rich anyway.

These ideas shaped my initial flawed perspective of money.

From the typical, educated American perspective, the path to success looks like this:

Borrow money for college.

Take a low-level position at a company and work your way up.

Get credit cards to build credit but try not to overuse them (end up overusing them anyway).

Borrow money to buy a car.

Borrow money to buy a house.

Delay gratification for the next thirty, forty, or fifty years. Put everything you can into savings. Drive that old car until it breaks down.

Borrow and save, borrow and save.

Even though I skipped the part about college, I was in the same rut as everyone else, but without a college degree. Any time I looked for a job with benefits, or one that paid modestly more than minimum wage, I found that most required at least a bachelor's degree. I had very little earning potential (or so I thought).

For someone wanting to break the cycle of poverty, I saw no hope.

When I was poor, I didn't think much about money, besides how badly I needed it or ways I could save more of the meager amount I was bringing in. If I had to describe my perspective on how money works or how people achieve success, my answer wouldn't have been very clear:

I assumed you were supposed to work hard until the person above you noticed and gave you a promotion. Then you'd keep working hard until eventually ending up wherever you were supposed to be. You'd get married, have kids, save up to take a week-long vacation once a year, and work to pay your bills until you retired. Then you'd read books and occasionally play golf.

Isn't that the way the system is set up?

Sure, occasionally some lucky person might have a brainstorm and come up with a brilliant idea that makes them a lot of money. Perhaps someone else would get really, really lucky in the stock market and could afford the luxuries they'd always wanted.

I didn't know how to do that. I didn't even know if there was a way to learn how to do that. So I kept working minimum-wage jobs, waiting for whatever was supposed to happen to happen.

Eventually I learned when you do that, what's supposed to happen is nothing.

WHERE DOES THIS PERSPECTIVE COME FROM?

Our perspective on money is shaped in large part by our experience in school.

School is a system, and an easy one to understand. If you work hard, you get an A on your report card. Get enough As, and you get to go to the college of your choice. In short, you win.

Some people might have an easier time studying than others, but ideally the system is designed so that anyone who works hard enough can get good grades.

You didn't have to think about how to succeed in school. If you did what you were told, you passed. If you didn't, you failed.

Is it surprising, then, that most people, after they graduate, expect the real world to work the same way?

Subconsciously, whether we admit it or not, a lot of us feel like there's a system and we should be guaranteed some level of success if we just follow the rules.

So we do what we're told: go to school, take on debt, get a job, buy a car, take on debt, buy a house, take on debt.

Somehow it never works out the way we expect. Most of us spend our lives making money for other people with little to show for it.

The problem is our schools don't teach us how to make money. Most of our parents don't teach us how to make money. Your boss won't teach you how to make money—in fact, everyone you work for is incentivized to give you as little money as possible so there's more money for them.

It's tempting to believe that the people above you have it all figured out. The truth is, your boss is just as worried about her next paycheck as you are.

For years, the US government pushed the idea of home ownership. It spent years convincing people it was the way to achieve the American Dream. We bought it because we believe there's a system that's going to take care of us the way our teachers did, the way our parents

14

did. If the system tells us to buy a house, then we're going to buy a house.

Prices went through the roof. People took out loans they couldn't afford. Financial advisors reassured their clients, telling them, "Home prices can only go up." The people above us kept saying it was a great idea, and we listened.

Then it all came crashing down. Foreclosures skyrocketed. Millions of people lost their homes. The stock market followed. Retirement accounts were wiped out.

All those people who played by the rules and did what they were told were left penniless.

There was a lot of blame to go around, but at the end of the day, so many people lost their life savings because this is the real world and nobody—*nobody*—knows what the rules are. There's no system, just a collection of people like you trying to do the best they can with what they have.

Some people are really bothered by this.

They blame the government, they blame corporations, they blame everything they think should be taking care of them.

The real problem is not in any of those places. Money works the way it does because of human nature.

Every generation, a few people decide to accept this fact of life and find ways to work with it, to use it to their advantage and carve out a better life for themselves and their families. They decide to take a grown-up view about money. In fact, understanding this basic feature of human nature is the first step to creating wealth.

Sadly, many other grown-ups chose not to take this view. They want the real world to work the way school does, where you're told when to show up and what to do to get your A.

They don't realize that, while schools generally don't go out of business, companies do all the time.

You can do everything right, then walk into work on a Tuesday morning and everything's gone. Then your paycheck bounces.

You can invest all your money in something "safe," only to have the market crash and all your savings vanish.

You might never see that pension you were promised.

Even assurances from the government aren't final—I hope you're not counting on that monthly Social Security check to get through your retirement.

In life, you can ace all the exams and still fail.

So what are we supposed to do if there's no set of rules to follow? How can we be financially secure, let alone rich, if doing things the way we're "supposed" to doesn't come with any guarantees?

What we need is a new way of thinking about money.

ME, BEFORE AND AFTER

I wanted the impossible.

I wanted to be rich while I was still young enough to enjoy it, but I didn't know how.

I was barely keeping my head above water and was living without the things I wanted. I couldn't take a vacation; I couldn't go out with friends; I couldn't spend money on anything that wasn't necessary for survival.

There were few choices. I could either take on more debt to enjoy life temporarily, or I could choose to live like I was even poorer than I already was so that someday way off in the future I could be financially secure.

Neither sounded like good options, so I kept doing what I was doing, scraping by and spending all my money every month, waiting for something to happen.

At my worst I was paying a few bucks a month to sleep on the living room floor of a friend's apartment. I had a twenty-year-old car that leaked oil almost as fast as I could put it in the engine. I couldn't afford to fix it. When it finally died I had to borrow a bicycle to get to work.

A few years after changing my perspective on money, I walked into a dealership and bought a Maserati with cash. (Okay, technically it was a check for the full amount.) I bought a house, rented it out for more than the mortgage, and then bought another house.

I didn't have to check my bank account before going to a nice restaurant. When I went out with friends, I could pick up the tab.

After changing my perspective on money, I finally got to travel and cross things off of my bucket list. Before long I was drinking Guinness in Dublin, eating pizza in Naples, riding camels in Africa, dancing flamenco in Barcelona, and playing baccarat in Monte Carlo.

Before my perspective changed, I worked the register at a McDonald's (I told my friends I had a job at a Fortune 500 company). I worked the concession stand at a movie theater and in the kitchen at a Taco Bell.

After my perspective on money changed, *Inc.* magazine added me to their list of the fastest growing multimillion dollar companies in America. I say "me"

17

because the company I founded had no other employees or investors. The company's office is wherever I have cell reception or Wi-Fi so I can check to make sure I'm still making money.

Before my perspective changed, I had no college degree or certifications.

After... well, I still have none of those things. Along the way I realized that putting "Certified Google AdWords Specialist" on a resume would take up space where I could have written "Profitably managed hundreds of millions of dollars in pay-per-click advertising."

You can guess which one a hiring manager cares more about.

None of that would have happened if I hadn't realized that the way everyone told me to think about money was wrong. I got to a point where something had to change. So I changed.

I CHANGED, AND I WON

Two years before I walked into my boss's office to ask for a $150,000 raise, I set a very immodest goal for myself.

I would double my income every twelve months.

I told myself I would do whatever it took, legally and ethically, to make it happen.

Why double?

I have a favorite story that I heard as a kid. There are several versions, but the one I heard went something like this:

A very wise man worked as an advisor to a wealthy king. When the wise man grew old, the king was worried his advisor's wits had been dulled by age. He called the advisor before him and offered the advisor any reward he wanted for his lifetime of service but told him that it was time for the wise man to retire. The advisor insisted the only reward he wanted was to continue serving the king. The king was unmoved, so the advisor asked for time to consider what reward to ask for.

After thinking it over, the wise man came back with a chessboard. He asked the king to send him a single grain of rice, while he pointed to the first square on the board. He told the king to send two grains of rice the next day, pointing to the second square, and four grains on the third day, doubling the amount of rice each day until all the squares were filled.

The king was shocked that the advisor would ask for so little but felt justified in forcing the man into retirement. After all, what person in their right mind would ask for a few grains of rice in exchange for a lifetime of service?

The king vowed to give the advisor his reward and sent him on his way.

There are 64 squares on a chessboard.

On the first day, the king sent a grain of rice, as promised.

On the second day, he sent 2 grains of rice.

On the third day, he sent 4 grains.

On the fourth day, he sent 8.

The fifth day was 16.

The sixth day was 32.

The seventh day was 64.

The eighth day was 128.

The pile of rice was growing, but at least one row was completed.

The ninth day, the king sent 256 grains.

On the tenth, 512.

The eleventh, 1,024.

The twelfth, 2,048.

The thirteenth, 4,096.

The fourteenth, 8,192.

The fifteenth, 16,384.

The sixteenth day, the king sent 32,768 grains of rice—slightly more than a pound. He was starting to worry, but still, what was a few pounds of rice?

Halfway through the third row, the number was up to 524,288, or about 18 pounds of rice. A few days later, the king had to hire more men to haul all the rice to the advisor's home.

By the time the king got to the fourth row, the shipment had grown to more than 500 pounds.

The king's treasurer brought him disturbing news. The entire wealth of the kingdom would be drained long before the chessboard was full.

The king summoned the wise man and pleaded to be released of his vow. The wise man agreed, on one condition—that he be allowed to continue in the king's service.

The king readily agreed.

If it had been possible to continue the shipments of rice, the amount of rice due on the final day would have been 18,446,744,073,709,551,615 grains, or 615 *trillion* pounds.

I've heard that Albert Einstein was once asked what he believed to be the most powerful force in the universe. After thinking a for a moment, he replied, "Compound interest."

The rice story is a good illustration of how fast wealth can grow—but good luck finding 100 percent interest rates. If you're a standard investor, your savings and investments might double every ten years or so.

The story also taught me why saving and investing is a much better tool for the wealthy to build more wealth than it is for the poor. If you start on the first row, the gains from day to day are hardly noticeable. In the case of rice, it's literally not enough to live on.

If you start on the fourth or fifth row, the gains are staggering.

Looking at it another way, I had one grain of rice to invest. I wanted thousands, and I didn't want to wait decades.

The solution was more income, and my goal was to increase mine as fast as possible. Using the model from the story, I set out to double my income every year.

I had no idea how to do it, but I promised myself I'd figure it out.

I did not want to be stuck in low-wage jobs all my life.

I did not want my future to be at the mercy of a careless employer.

I did not want my family's safety to be determined by the up- and downturns of the economy.

And I was so sick of eating ramen.

I wasn't going to ask my friends or family for input, and for a very important reason: the few people I did tell my plan to looked at me like I was crazy.

Many of them even got mad.

They were still listening to the voice that says, *No, play it safe*.

We're all deeply conditioned on how to think about money, to the point where we don't want others to succeed *too much*. You'll run into this issue a lot. Many people will see your desire to get ahead as a character flaw, regardless of your motivations.

So I struck out alone. I worked for myself on nights and weekends. I researched. I experimented. I tried many different ways of earning extra income, from writing to sales to marketing. I failed a lot.

I missed my free time, but I stuck it out. I was putting in countless hours for almost no return. I would read more and work harder, but nothing would happen.

I didn't know it at the time, but with every failure I was learning a new secret to making money.

DO IT

When I set my goal to double my income every year, I was only making $14,000 annually. I knew I was aiming high, but I believed it was better to aim high and miss, and there was no harm in trying.

When I walked into my boss's office to ask for a 200 percent raise, I was already ahead of schedule. I had turned that $14,000 into $72,000 and had finally caught up to my high school classmates. There was also no student loan debt coming out of my paycheck.

It still wasn't where I wanted to be. My financial future was still out of my control. What if I lost the job tomorrow?

In life, there's always risk. Nowhere is that more obvious than in personal finances. You can never eliminate the risk, but you can reduce it, and the best way to reduce financial risk is to have more money. I had to have enough so it wouldn't matter if I got fired. I had to have enough money so that losing a job wouldn't mean losing my ability to support my family.

I worked hard on the pitch. This was the deciding moment. I used everything I'd learned about making money over the previous two years and poured it all into preparing for that one conversation.

It turned out to be the most important moment in my financial life.

It was a turning point that taught me, once and for all, that everything I used to believe about money was wrong.

All the advice I'd been given about money my whole life never came close to getting me out of the cycle of poverty.

When my perspective changed, I realized there was only one rule that mattered. It wasn't what grades you got or where you went to school or what you invested in.

It was the single most important rule of making money.

I got the raise. All six figures of it. In twenty minutes, I'd done more for my career than any of my friends had done in four years of college.

That makes some people mad. It should. It should make you mad that everything you've been told about making money and getting ahead still won't get you further than one twenty-minute conversation.

When I realized it was all wrong, I was livid—for a moment. Then I used it as motivation to continue learning. I suggest you do so as well.

While I still haven't achieved the same success as that storied wise man, changing my perspective allowed me to double my income again and again.

All told, I doubled my income seven times in seven years.

If you want to get an idea of how large of an increase that is, get a calculator and type in your current salary, then multiply it by two seven times.

In this book I'll tell you how I negotiated that raise, and how you can win the next time you sit down to ask for more money.

I'll also tell you how I managed to stop working for other people and become my own boss, and how I made more money than I'd ever dreamed of—all while in my pajamas.

My change in perspective allowed me to view money in a new light. It let me see the reasons why things happened the way they did when it came to money.

It's allowed me to succeed as an employee and later as an entrepreneur, creating a company that brings in millions of dollars a year.

The success I've had reads just like those scammy get-rich-quick ads. I make money while I sleep. I work from my couch. I travel the world while passive income streams make money for me.

I can spend as much time as I want with my kids (which is a lot—they're the funniest people I know).

I'm going to tell you how I did it.

First, though, you're going to have to change your perspective on money.

You're going to have to forget what you've been told so I can teach you what I wish I'd been taught decades ago.

There's only one hard rule about making money. Beyond that, the rest is a game, and I'm going to teach you how to play it.

CHAPTER 2

MISCONCEPTIONS

The first thing we need to do is clear up some common misconceptions. These won't all apply to you, but most of us have picked up a few of these along the way.

THESE PEOPLE ARE NOT YOUR FRIENDS

The best way to start is to learn who your financial friends are. This is very easy to do, because when you're poor, you don't have any.

Don't worry, I'm going to tell you how to turn each of these financial enemies into an ally. (Spoiler: it involves having more money.)

Credit card companies are not your friends.

The most important thing to remember is that credit is not your money. A lot of young people make the mistake of thinking that having a new $500-limit credit card means they have an extra $500 to spend. If you didn't have $500 before you got the credit card, you don't have $500 after you get the card.

Credit is a short-term loan that can turn into a disaster if you don't pay it off in time. When you're rich, you'll be able to use these free loans to actually generate more income for yourself. For now, keep in mind that, as long as you pay your bill in full every month, credit card companies legally can't charge you interest.

Like I said, however, credit card companies are not your friends. They want you to mess up. Just one missed payment can create a ripple effect and cause you to rack up massive fees and charges. Remember compound interest? Don't let it work against you.

Treat your credit card like you would a debit card that pulls money directly out of your bank account. If you don't have the money in your account right now to buy what you want, don't use the credit card.

When you're rich, the credit card companies are your friends. They pay me thousands of dollars a year just to use their cards because merchants have to pay them transaction fees anytime I spend money, and I spend a lot of money. I've spent the past few years traveling all over the world for free thanks to credit card rewards. If you're poor, don't use a credit card. If you're rich, find a good one and use it all the time.

The bank is not your friend.

When you're rich, banks will want to be your friend. They will bend over backward to give you money. They'll waive fees and offer free services. When you're poor, though, you are a revenue source to be exploited.

Think of it this way: If I put $100,000 in the bank, they can loan it out and make thousands of dollars a year in interest. If your bank account has an average balance of $100, the bank isn't making much in interest, so they're going to have to find other ways to make money off of you.

Getting a new customer is expensive for a bank, and they will do anything they can to get a return on their investment. They will charge you to use ATMs, charge you overdraft fees and minimum-balance fees, or even charge you for making too many visits to the bank in a month.

Shop around. Find a bank with the fewest fees and learn the rules. The last thing you want is to be charged for not having enough money in your account. It's expensive to be poor.
When you have more money, the fees will go away because the bank wants your business and they won't drive you away by nickel-and-diming you.

Your boss is not your friend.

Your boss might be a wonderful person. Maybe you're even lucky enough to have one who actually cares about you. Keep one thing in mind, though: bosses are incentivized to get the most work out of you for the smallest cost to the business.

When you're the boss, you'll have the same incentive.

You'll try to rise above it, but you have bills to pay, too, and the business's bottom line will always put pressure on your decisions. Keeping your employees happy is good business, but if you're more generous than the company can afford, everyone is going to end up unemployed.

Your boss and the company you work for are not interested in helping you improve your life.

Maybe your company offers great benefits. Perhaps they offer you money to further your education. Of course, this isn't so you can become more qualified and land a job somewhere else. It almost always comes with requirements forcing you to stay with the company for a certain number of years or else you have to pay back the cost of tuition. You can still use these programs to your advantage; just remember that, from your employer's perspective, it's a way to keep you from leaving.

Most people offering investment advice are not your friends.

Seems like if you can't get rich on your own, there's money in trying to tell other people how to get rich.

This quote from Warren Buffett sums it up nicely: "Wall Street is the only place that people ride to in a Rolls-Royce to get advice from those who take the subway."

Stock advice is one of the oldest rackets in the game. Some advisors will promise to teach your their "system" for making millions in the stock market. Sure, it's possible to make a lot of money actively trading stocks. It's far more likely that you'll lose money very quickly. If you don't already have money you can afford to lose, you shouldn't be picking stocks. Investing in a solid mutual fund or exchange-traded fund that's indexed to the S&P 500 is a better place to park your money.

Be skeptical of overly optimistic scenarios.

Yes, the stock market can give you average annual returns of 10 percent or more. That's an average, and if you've got the time to spare and can wait a few decades you'll likely see similar returns. However, if you'd invested in an S&P fund in 2000, you'd have had less money by 2010 than you started with. Know the risks before you hand over your money.

Most solid investments are great if you're rich, have money to spare and don't need to make a profit anytime soon. If you don't already have a decent amount of money, these kind of investments are not for you.

If you're poor, the best investment you can make is paying off your debts.

PAY OFF BAD DEBTS BEFORE INVESTING

I'm often asked by people with low-paying jobs and very little money what I think they should invest in to get rich. They want a hot stock tip to take their $500 and turn it into a fortune. Most people in that situation have no business investing in stocks.

Many Americans live paycheck to paycheck. Nearly two-thirds have no emergency savings. Forty percent do not have a positive net worth.

It's sad to think that even when I was barely scraping by on $14,000 a year, I was still wealthier than 40 percent of Americans as long as I had $1 in my pocket.

Often, that was all I had. Fortunately, even when I was clueless about money, I managed to stay away from unsecured debt. (It was actually easy because nobody would give me a credit card.)

Don't even think about investing if you have high-interest credit card debt. Paying down high-interest loans has better guaranteed returns than any investment out there.

There's an important distinction to make here, though. Certain kinds of debt can be a great investment.

While some people rack up a ton of credit card debt, other people have the misconception that *all* debt is bad.

CERTAIN KINDS OF DEBT CAN BE A GREAT WAY TO BUILD WEALTH

We'll get into investing using debt later, but first I want to tell you about an interesting trick with debt the rich use to both make money and avoid paying taxes.

Say you owned $100 million worth of stock and wanted to buy a yacht. You could sell some stock to buy the yacht, but then you'd have to pay taxes on your earnings. Also, you'd lose out on dividends and appreciation on your investment. Leaving the money where it is gets you an average return of 10 percent a year. If you can use the stock as collateral to get a low rate on a loan—say 5 percent—it makes sense not to sell your stock. Your investment will make money faster than the loan will generate interest, so you'll actually come out ahead in the long run.

So instead of selling stock, you borrow the money instead, buy your yacht, keep your investment, and don't have to pay taxes. On top of that, there are some cases where you can even write off loan interest. For the wealthy, there's very little reason to sell your assets to pay for anything. Debt can be used in place of income whenever they want something. Meanwhile, the government takes nothing because the investment gain is never realized, so there's nothing to tax.

Does your credit card debt do that?

It's counterintuitive, but you should never go into debt until you have money. In the meantime, if you are

31

going to use a credit card, find one that gives you cash back and pay it off every month. If you never miss a payment, you'll be getting a 1 to 5 percent discount on everything you buy.

COLLEGE

Anyone telling you that you have to go to college no matter what is not your friend.

People will tell you that college is an investment, and that's true, but not all investments are good investments. Do your due diligence and weigh your options. Four years and $150,000 in loans for a $40,000 starting salary and not much room for growth is a terrible investment.

Many young adults still think someone is going to stop them from making a bad decision. After eighteen years of being told what to do, they wonder, *Why would I be allowed to do this if it's a bad idea?* Worse, in many cases they're actually encouraged to make these kinds of terrible investments.

Welcome to adulthood, where there are an infinite amount of bad ideas and very few people to tell you to stay away from them.

It's unfortunate that people have to make what may be the biggest financial decision of their lives while they're still teenagers. What's downright cruel is that we don't even teach them how to make the decision. A public education will teach you almost nothing about making money.

School gives us the skills to perform a certain job, but it doesn't teach us how to be successful.

Education is extremely important, and you should always be learning and challenging yourself. However, always ask yourself if what you're learning is going to help you make money, or just help you make money for other people.

If I'd gone to college, I would have learned how to be an employee, gotten a decent job, worked for forty years, and had a nice little retirement. Skipping college made it harder for me to get jobs and forced me to learn ways to make money for myself, not for a boss.

College is an excellent choice for many people, and in most cases it's the right one, but it's certainly not the only choice.

HOME OWNERSHIP

Whether you go to college or not, at some point you'll likely want to buy your own home. Contrary to what the realtor and mortgage broker will tell you, your house is not a great investment.

In 2007, many people were still promoting the idea that you should buy the most expensive house you could afford.

"It's a great investment and only goes up in value."

In fact, some of the people saying this were the ones giving out the loans. They'd give you the money and then they'd sell your loan to another bank and place a big bet on the side that you wouldn't be able to pay your mortgage.

These people were not anyone's friend.

Your home is closer to a savings account than a true income-generating investment.

If you're very lucky, the value of your house will go up and cover the cost of maintenance, taxes, and all the extra interest you'll pay to the bank over the next thirty years.

If you break even at the end of the mortgage, it'll be like living rent free for decades. That's nice, but good investments actually make money for you.

Here's an example. Say you're doing well later in life and want to buy a single-family home for $500,000. Interest rates today are still low, but it'll still likely cost you twice the price of the house by the time you're done paying it off. Owning a house can also mean expensive repairs that you wouldn't be on the hook for if you were renting.

I found this out the hard way. A week after we moved into our current house, my son "accidentally" flushed one of his toy cars down the toilet. It caught in a pipe leading away from the house. $5,000 and a torn-up backyard later, we were still cleaning up the mess from all the backed-up toilets.

It's not a stretch to assume the house will go up in value enough to cover these costs, so you may come out even, but the goal of an investment is to make money.

Instead of buying that house for $500,000, consider what would happen if you bought two town houses for $250,000 each. You could live in one and rent out the other.

Depending on the market, the rent income would probably be slightly above or slightly below what you're paying on the mortgage, so we'll call it even. After thirty years, the house you live in might be worth all the money you've put into it, similar to a savings account. The second house is worth just as much, but someone else put in the money.

The end result of the first scenario is that you got to live rent free for thirty years.

The end result of the second scenario is that you got to live rent free for thirty years and got a free house out of it.

I did something similar when I bought my second house. The first home I bought was a town house that I paid for with a no-money-down, 100 percent mortgage (back when those still existed) at a low rate. A few years later, I was doing well and had some new tiny roommates who needed extra space. Instead of selling the town house and buying the biggest home I could afford, I bought a smaller house than I could afford and rented out the town house. I was able to charge more in rent than the cost of the mortgage.

Since I put no money down on the town house and now have renters more than covering expenses, when the mortgage term ends, I'll get a free home. The bank bought the house, my renters paid the bank, and I get the house.

With even a modest 3 percent growth rate on the price of the house, it will be worth over a million dollars by the time I hit retirement age, and I didn't have to put down a dime. That's a free million-dollar retirement fund.

That's a good investment.

GOVERNMENT

The government is not your friend, and it's a terrible source for financial advice.

For years, the US government tried to get everyone to buy a house. Conventional wisdom said it was the best way to achieve the American Dream. That it's a great investment because housing prices only ever go up.

Millions of foreclosures later, people finally realized that not everyone is at a point in their life where home ownership makes sense.

For years there's been a huge push to get everyone to go to college, regardless of the cost. Americans now owe more than a trillion dollars in student loan debt. That's more than all the credit card debt in the country combined, and could very well be the next bubble to burst.

The government may seem like a friend when you're poor, but once you make the decision to escape poverty and get ahead, it will actively hinder you. Oddly enough, once you become super rich, the government will be your friend again—or at least leave you alone.

Let's look at how the government "helps" you save for your retirement. The idea behind Social Security sounds great: the government will take care of you when you get older. For decades, it was actually a pretty good deal for workers who paid into it.

However, the current math shows that if things aren't fixed many young people today will get paid out much less when they retire than they put in during their working years. They might actually be better off burying their money in their backyard. Of course, the government doesn't give you that option.

When you're poor, the government does offer a lot of programs to try to help you deal with poverty. However, as you focus on getting ahead and put in the work to build wealth, the government is there to take its cut. The more successful you are, the larger percentage of your income the government takes from you. It adds up fast.

Here in the United States, a highly successful employee or small business owner can wind up with more than half her income going to federal, state, and local government taxes. If you do manage to beat the odds on the path to building wealth, the government will make more from it than you will.

Of course the rules change when you're super rich. I'm not talking about the top 1 percent—more like the top 0.01 percent.

Remember the trick about the yacht? Income tax isn't really an issue when you already have obscene amounts of money, because there are ways to get and spend money that the government doesn't tax as income. Even capital gains taxes can be creatively avoided. It's very disingenuous when people who are already wealthy come out in favor of raising income taxes on high earners. They get a lot of praise because they're willing to "pay their fair share," but the reality is the income tax rate could be 100 percent, and it wouldn't affect them at all. Net worth taxes (which are extremely rare and don't exist in the United States) are taxes on the rich. The income tax is a tax on people *trying to become* rich.

When you're poor, the government helps you; when you're rich, it mostly leaves you alone, but if you're in the middle trying to work your way up, it'll force you to work even harder.

INVESTORS

Once you've decided to take control of your financial future, you'll likely want to start your own business. Keep in mind that investors are not your friends.

Yes, in some cases, they are necessary and can bring a lot of experience and connections to the table. It could very well be worth it to bring them on board. Depending on the business, you might have no other choice.

Even if they are necessary, they are still not your friends. They are in it to make money. They care about your success only as far as it gets them paid. Bringing on investors means giving up total control of your business and splitting any potential profit.

Some businesses need a lot of capital to start with because they need to reach a certain scale to function properly, and in those cases, having investors is unavoidable.

You don't need to start one of these businesses.

Many people have the misconception that starting a business is expensive, but it doesn't have to be. I started my first multimillion dollar company with $6,000 that I put on a credit card (but not before I could afford to pay it off).

Starting a company used to require a lot of capital. It would generally involve opening a storefront and paying for physical space, physical inventory, and hiring employees, all of which are expensive. With only one store, you could only sell to a limited number of people in a local area. With the internet, you can have a store up tonight for a few bucks and sell to anyone in the world. Technology has made it easier than ever to start a business with very little capital.

I've run many businesses from my laptop with no employees. I've never taken on an investor. I've never held physical inventory. I can work from anywhere in the world, without deadlines or having to manage employees, and without worrying about paying off a large business loan.

If you design a scalable business that's easy to automate, you greatly reduce your need for investors and give yourself a lot more freedom.

HARD WORK AND MONEY

There are several misconceptions about how hard work relates to making money. You've probably been taught some of these misconceptions by people who find it easier to blame their circumstances than to change them. Some believe that successful people didn't earn their wealth, they're just better at lying and stealing than the rest of us.

While that's certainly true in some cases, most successful people did earn their wealth, and they did it through hard work (just not necessarily at their day job, as I'll explain in a second).

A similar misconception is the belief that most rich people inherited their wealth. Since success in life is determined at birth, nobody can be blamed for their financial situation.

This is a cop-out. Nearly all fortunes in the United States are made in a single lifetime. Don't sit around blaming the sperm lottery; get out there and work for what you want.

On the flip side, there will always be people who believe hard work is the *only* requirement for success. They think that as long as you have a good work ethic, eventually you'll be able to build wealth.

Some of the hardest-working people in the world are also the poorest.

Hard work on its own won't make you successful. It's a good way to speed up your journey to financial success, but if you're not pointed in the right direction, it doesn't matter how fast you're going.

Success is not about how hard you work, it's about how hard you work to get ahead.

You can put in backbreaking work for sixty hours a week, but if you aren't working hard to get ahead, you could end up doing that same work for fifty years of your life.

"If one does not know to which port one is sailing, no wind is favorable."
—Seneca

Think of hard work as wind in your sails. You won't get anywhere without it, but if it's just blowing you in circles, you're wasting your time. Before you commit to putting in all those extra hours, make sure you know which direction you're going. Working hard for other people will only get you so far. You need to learn how to work hard for yourself.

CLIPPING COUPONS

When you're poor, figuring out how to spend your time is easy. Let's look at a simple decision: if you see your lawn needs mowing, you mow it.

When you're making good money, these kind of decisions require more math. Let's assume you're now a business consultant making $300 an hour and you've got more than enough clients to keep you busy. If mowing your lawn takes an hour and you can hire someone to do it for $30, it would actually cost you $270 to mow your own lawn. You're saving $30, but you're losing out on the $300 of income you could have brought in by doing an hour of your primary work.

If you love to get out there in your yard and do manual labor with your bare hands, then by all means go do it. Just keep in mind that you're paying for the privilege. When I hear stories about ultra-rich people clipping coupons, I always scratch my head.

It's not a praiseworthy example of frugality. Sure, it's sometimes necessary when you're poor, but for the extremely rich, clipping coupons is a bad and expensive habit.

"It's free money," they'll say, holding a paper square worth 50 cents off a can of baked beans they never would have bought without the coupon. "If you saw a penny on the ground, you wouldn't leave it there, would you?"

If there were ten thousand pennies on the ground, and I stopped to pick them all up, I still wouldn't have enough money to pay for the surgery I'd need to fix my back.

I once watched a woman spend two hours trying to find the cheapest oil change in town. She called every gas station in the area. In the end, she drove to the other side of town and saved $5. How much money can you earn in two to three hours? More than $5.

People actually try to sell the idea that these are the habits that make people wealthy. It's true that frugality can be a wonderful trait and help you immensely, but there's a point where it should stop.

If you put in the same amount of effort toward the big things as you do the small things, you'd get a lot further. Spending ten more minutes negotiating the contract on your first home can save you more than an entire lifetime of coupon clipping.

RISK

Many people believe that being an entrepreneur is risky. They think it's much safer to go to college, get a good job, and do things the "right" way.

The truth is, there's no financial path that doesn't involve risk. Even the "safest" options are risky, because life is risky.

If you're an employee, you're counting on the people in charge to make enough good decisions to keep the company profitable and make sure the paychecks go out on time.

Working for someone else is not less risky. You just have the luxury of not seeing the risk every day.

When you're the boss, the decisions that will grow your company or lead it to bankruptcy are in your hands. You are forced to deal with the risk every day, but you have something the average employee doesn't have—control.

If you don't own the company, you can't stop bad decisions that will have a negative impact on the company's bottom line or its employees. You can't stop a decision to, say, outsource all of the company's jobs to China.

You have to trust your job will still be around every morning while you commute to work. You have to trust that there's enough money in the bank to pay your salary.

People get laid off. Entire industries disappear. Skill sets that were once in demand become useless. There is no guarantee that your safe path will still exist tomorrow or next year.

By becoming an entrepreneur, you'll learn how to find new paths. A change in the economy won't be a setback—it will be an opportunity to earn your fortune.

Yes, it involves risk, but at least you get to be the one steering the ship.

There's one last misconception I want to address, and it's a big one.

Being rich will not solve your problems.

It won't make you a better person. It won't make all your relationship issues disappear. If you had character flaws before, if anything, being rich might make them worse.

Money doesn't buy happiness. It can free you from a lot worry and stress, but the happiness is something you have to find on your own.

Being rich won't solve all your problems.

It will, however, solve your money problems.

And that's pretty freakin' sweet.

43

CHAPTER 3

THE ONLY RULE OF MAKING MONEY

I remember when I became an adult and finally realized that adults, like kids, have no idea what they're doing. It took me awhile to figure out that this also applied to money.

It's not a set system.

Changing your perspective on money means realizing that there's no scheme, order, or organization waiting to reward you for doing the "right things." Making more money is not about how good of an employee you are. It's not about how hard you work at your job. It's about how hard you work at getting ahead.

I've worked for as little as 50 cents an hour. I've had five-minute conversations that have made me hundreds of thousands of dollars. Money doesn't care how hard you work.

We're taught that if we don't do things the "right way," we're taking risks with our future. We're not taught that there's risk in everything and that life is about balancing risk and reward. When I was younger, I thought that starting a business was risky. I even thought that leaving a cushy but low-paying job was risky.

Now, I think risk is leaving your fate in the hands of a business you have no control over, hoping they'll continue to appreciate your work and believing they'll always have enough money in the bank to cover your paycheck.

Too often, they don't.

You can't eliminate risk. You can start a healthy diet and get hit by a car tomorrow. You can do what you're told is safe and go to college, take on hundreds of thousands of dollars of debt, buy a house you can't afford, struggle to find work, and end up declaring personal bankruptcy.

One of the best steps you can take to reduce financial risk is to be wealthy. That sounds obvious, but it's not in most people's financial plan for their lives. Instead, they plan on doing things the "safe" way, which pretty much guarantees they'll never be wealthy.

I've met a lot of really smart people who can't figure out how to make money. If they can't do it, what hope do the rest of us have?

Too many choices leads to paralysis. It's not that there's no way to make money. It's that there are too many ways.

There are so many options it's daunting, so many people choose the path nobody will fault them for. If you skip college to start a business and the business fails, then everyone thinks you made a dumb decision. If you go to college and end up with loads of debt and a mediocre job, it's poor luck or the economy's fault.

Instead of following the supposedly safe path that's laid out for you, I propose an exercise.

Sit down somewhere quiet with a pen and a piece of paper. Work out how much money you'd need to make per year to live the life you want. I'm not talking limos and private jets, but pick a number that the eighteen-year-old version of yourself wouldn't be upset to see in your shared future.

This isn't your normal budgeting. Stop trying to make your current income fit your existing bills. Instead, put together the bills you want. Come up with all the things you reasonably want to be able to afford.

When you have the list, compare it to what you currently make.

How much more money do you need to be able to pay for those things?

Is it a number you can reach by working for someone else?

If so, great; I'll tell you the best strategies to make that happen.

If not, keep reading, and I'll let you in on the secrets of wealth creation that took me from $14,000 a year to millions. It's not the safe path that everyone else tells you to take, the one that looks like:

Spend less than you make.
Invest a little bit every month.
Make your money work for you.

What money? People aren't reading books about making money because they have money to invest. They're looking for financial advice because they're poor.

When I was making $14,000 a year, I spent a lot of time thinking about ways to save money. I did everything I could to spend less than I made. I lived off of 39-cent burritos and ramen noodles from the local grocery store that I walked to in order to save gas money. It was as bad as it sounds.

46

When my perspective changed, I spent that time thinking about how to make more money. If you don't make much, you can't save much. If you're poor, you'll never be able to save your way to wealth. I could never have saved myself into the position I'm in now, even if I'd been able to invest 100 percent of my income. There has to be a better way.

THE RULE

It would be a lot easier if getting rich was a simple ten-step process. If someone tries to sell you a ten-step process to getting rich, they are selling you a scam that will get them rich, not you.

The purpose of this chapter isn't to teach you a step-by-step list of the things to do to become wealthy. It's to teach you the one rule of money and how to apply it. The purpose of this chapter is to change how you think about creating wealth.

Learn the rule. Learn the new way to think about money. Change your perspective.

There's only one rule to ethically making money in a free market. It is not "go to college." It is not "follow your passion." It's not "buy real estate."

The only rule to making money is this:

Create value.

Or a more applicable version:

Figure out what someone wants, then find a way to give it to them.

47

This is equally true if you're trying to get a raise, find a new job, or sell your product to more customers. To make more money, you need to figure out what people want and give it to them.

Adding value is not the same as working harder. As an affiliate marketer, I add value to other companies by bringing them customers at a lower cost than their internal marketing teams. As a reward, I keep a chunk of the cost savings. Since I'm able to automate most of the marketing processes I use, I can add considerable value with very little effort.

It's not always enough to just create value. You have to show it. That's why investment bankers earn far more than teachers and many doctors—when the person above you sees a bunch of money coming in next to your name on a spreadsheet, it's easier to justify ridiculous salaries.

As an employee, showing value is just as important as creating it. Someone else gets to decide what you're worth, so they need to be convinced of the value you bring to the table.

People in sales earn more because they're closer to the money. The value they add is easier to translate into a dollar amount. I've worked at a lot of companies with very talented designers and programmers, but it was always the sales guys making the most money—even though what they were selling wouldn't exist without the designers and programmers.

It's much easier for someone in sales to demonstrate a specific monetary value for their work. When a deal closes to sell a software package for millions of dollars, the salesman who spent the past few weeks sealing the deal is going to be at the front of the CEO's mind—not the team of programmers who spent a year developing the software.

Realizing this, I looked for jobs where the value I added to a company was easily quantifiable. With no college degree or relevant experience, it was a struggle—I had to make several lateral moves and beg for more responsibility with each new job that I could add to my resume.

After sending my resume out a few hundred times, I was hired as an executive assistant at a biometrics company. They had a system that let people tie their bank info to their fingerprint, so instead of swiping a credit card to pay for groceries, customers could put their finger on a scanner and the bill was paid automatically.

Among other things, my job was to bring coffee to meetings. I asked my boss if I could stay and listen, then I took notes and asked my boss questions afterward. I made a few suggestions, most of which were dismissed, but it showed I was interested in taking on an increased role.

The company had a reseller program that paid affiliates to sell its fingerprint scanners. I asked if I could join the program and sell the product in my free time on the weekends. After walking all over town trying to convince restaurants, grocery stores, and any other business I came across to put one of our fingerprint readers by their register, I learned two things.

First, I learned that I suck at sales—I sold a total of zero units. I also learned enough about the product that they put me in charge of the reseller program.

I like to think it was because they were impressed with my entrepreneurial attitude, but the truth is, it was a start-up, nobody at the company wanted to run it, and they didn't want to hire someone for the job. It was more work and didn't come with a pay increase.

People who think about money in the normal way would have complained. I was excited. When I left the company, I didn't have to write "guy who brought the coffee to meetings," on my resume. I was an affiliate manager. I created go-to market plans. I could show value.

Eventually I landed a job in marketing where a substantial portion of my pay was directly tied to how much extra revenue I generated for the company.

That's when I asked for the $150,000 raise. After a year with the company, I could point to the tens of millions of dollars I had made or saved the business. Because I could show my added value in a way that was easily understood by anyone above me who might object, $150,000 was a small price to pay if it meant I would continue to bring in millions for the company.

I didn't get a $150,000 raise because I'm a smooth talker. In fact, I didn't say much at all. I'm pretty sure I was sweating and stuttering through the whole interaction. I presented hard numbers and let them do the talking.

People who think there's some kind of system or "right way" of doing things will get a job and suffer through it for a few years until they can't take it anymore. They'll quit and then look for something else, hopefully one that pays a bit more. If they're smart, they'll at least start the job search before walking out.

People who put themselves in charge of their own success will get a job, work hard at it, learn all they can, and constantly update their resume.

On the weekends, they'll check for job listings even if they enjoy where they are currently. They'll apply to jobs they'd never consider if they were unemployed, jobs they want but are unlikely to get. If they keep it up, eventually they'll get a phone call.

I applied to jobs paying double my current salary. I applied to VP positions. I applied to C-level positions. It didn't matter if I had the relevant experience if I believed I could do the job. Sure, I annoyed the crap out of HR managers, but that's not my problem.

I was always honest. Though I painted my skills in the best light possible, I never made anything up or invented credentials I didn't have. I never lied about how much I made with my current employer.

Since I already had a job and wasn't expecting another one, I could ask for whatever ludicrous salary I wanted.

You don't need to win all the time if the wins you do get are big. I got offers. These were jobs that I'd never dreamed I'd be doing for money I'd never dreamed I'd make. If you're already employed, you've got nothing to lose by e-mailing your resume a few dozen times every weekend.

The rule of creating value applies to every money situation. A boss is happy to give you a raise if she can see how it will make her more money. A creditor will negotiate debt if he believes doing so will get him something rather than nothing. A company will pay a lot of money to someone who can increase their sales. Customers will pay a premium if you deliver value.

ISN'T WANTING MONEY GREEDY?

I grew up in a conservative working-class setting. Wealth was looked down on. There was a certain nobility to poverty and a life of hard work. If someone was rich, people thought they'd probably cheated and abandoned their morals to get ahead.

It's easier to believe that anyone who has it better than you do is paying for it in some way. That attitude keeps a lot of people poor. The truth is, earned wealth is not a vice, nor is working hard to get ahead.

Money is not good or bad. Money is choices. The more money you have, the more choices you have.

You may be thinking about the mansion you're going buy when you get rich. Maybe you're thinking about lavish parties, attractive partners, or traveling the world. Maybe it's early retirement and playing a lot of golf.

You might also be thinking about the good you could do if you were rich. To you, that might mean helping your local church feed the homeless or having the time and money to finally be able to volunteer and build houses in poverty-stricken areas.

Money is options.

You can make more choices for yourself, and more choices that affect other people. Poverty isn't virtuous, poverty is a lack of choice. Choosing to stay in poverty out of a belief that pursuing wealth is evil is choosing to let other people make important decisions, letting other people decide what's right and wrong, who to help and who to ignore.

Money is responsibility, because wealth amplifies the effect of your actions. Bill Gates is able to accomplish more good than thousands of people could hope to achieve in their lifetimes. Some people don't want the responsibility.

> "Greed...is good"
> —Gordon Gekko

That's an oft-quoted movie line, usually by someone who doesn't share the sentiment. Humans have a love-hate relationship with greed. We're okay with people working hard to get ahead, as long as it's not ahead of us. I used to be solidly in the "greed is bad" camp. Coincidentally, I also used to be very poor.

Perhaps greed is so hated because we associate it with bad behaviors like theft. We picture workaholics who would rather make more money than spend time with family. Greedy people only think about themselves and money.

Now I see greed in much the same way as I see fear and anger. Like most emotions, it's not the feeling itself that is good or bad, but the actions it leads you to take.

I'm not greedy because I want to be a workaholic, I'm greedy because I want to be wealthy enough to spend less time working and more time with friends and family.
I want to be rich so I don't have to be a workaholic.

I'm not greedy because I like thinking about money, I'm greedy because I want to be wealthy enough that I don't need to be worried about money ever again. There's so much life to enjoy, but the constant fear of getting another bill you can't pay robs you of much of that enjoyment.

I'm not greedy because I love money, I'm greedy because I don't want money to have the power over me it held when I was poor.

Greed is one of the best motivators in the world. Instead of feeling bad about it, use your own greed to get to where you need to be.

You want a nice car? That's greed—use that desire to force you to take the steps to improve your financial situation.

I've used my own greed to provide for my family. We have a nice house in a good school district. We have health insurance. My kids don't have the same worries I had growing up. Our family never has to wonder where the next meal is coming from. When it's time for college, I can help with tuition if they decide to go. If I still thought greed was bad and that I should be happy with a meager existence, none of that would have happened.

Greed made me take responsibility for my own financial situation. I didn't have to hurt any puppies. No morals were trampled.

Some people don't like greed because it goes against the view of the world they've been sold since they were kids. They believe the system is supposed to take care of you. You show up every day and do what you're supposed to do. You gradually work your way up by following the rules. After a few decades, you're rewarded with a comfortable retirement.

That's not how it works.

In the real world you get laid off. You get passed over for a promotion because of office politics. Your paycheck bounces. The company you work for goes under. You get sick and can't work. Even if none of those things happen, you're stuck working for someone else for forty or fifty years of your life, with no control over your future, hoping to retire on Social Security checks which may or may not come.

Working your way up the ladder is tough, especially when those above you seldom offer to help. It's easy to look at them with contempt and blame a system based on greed.

It's harder to realize that the person above you on the ladder is just like you. It's not that they don't want to help you. It's not that they don't like you. It's that they're every bit as terrified as you are. They're one car accident, one health emergency, one bad report away from a financial meltdown. They have to keep showing up to work every day, even though there's a hundred other things they'd rather be doing.

The same is true for everyone on the ladder. Karma's not waiting to reward you for doing the right thing, going to college like you've been told to do, getting a safe job and showing up every day in the hopes of getting ahead.

Regardless of what we've all been told, that's not how the system works. It's not how it was designed, because the system *wasn't designed*. The market is a hodgepodge of ideas and people trying to get by and make what they can for themselves and their families.

It's important to understand this or you'll be fighting an uphill battle your whole life. Once you figure it out, instead of fighting the system, you can use it to your advantage.

Instead of blaming your boss, take the time to understand your boss's motivation. If you've got your own business, try to understand the motivation of the company you're looking to do business with. Ask yourself these two questions:

> *What do they want?*
> *How can I give it to them in a way that lets me get what I want?*

In other words, apply greed to the one rule of money and create value for others. Everyone needs something. See things from other people's point of view. Give them what they want so they'll give you what you want: money.

It's the heart of capitalism. At its uncorrupted best, it takes human greed and turns it into something good. The greedier you are, the more you have to help others.

PEOPLE WILL WANT YOU TO FAIL

The same people who believe in doing things the safe way are the ones who will want you to fail. Yes, they'll root for you, but only to a point.

Imagine you and your best friend have been overweight your whole lives.

You notice her losing a few pounds. You're legitimately happy for her. Then she loses a few more. Your happiness fades and is replaced by jealousy. You try sabotage.

"Here, eat this donut, you deserve it."

When that doesn't work, you start to rationalize.

I'd lose weight, too, if I had time to go to the gym.

The jealousy builds as she continues to lose weight.

She's not better than me.

She must be bulimic.

Your brain will throw out anything it can just so it doesn't have to think about the harsh reality—that the only differences between you and your friend are your own life choices.

You'll encounter a similar reaction when you tell people your financial plans. Mention that you're planning on starting a business and they'll wish you luck and mean it. They'll want you to do well—just not *too* well.

When I was younger and people asked me about my career goals, I'd tell them my goal was to become a billionaire. I stopped saying it after I noticed several people become visibly upset. Some were even angry. Perhaps they thought I was greedy. Maybe they thought I cared too much about money.

To me, setting such a high goal made perfect sense. If I worked hard to achieve it but only made it 1 percent of the way to my goal, I'd still be very well off. I'd be able to take care of my family and live comfortably without worrying about money.

If my goal was to be a dentist and I made it 1 percent of the way, I'd be in trouble.

Too many people shoot for mediocre. Some are sad when they miss it; the rest are sad when they hit it.

For some, just hearing somebody talk about lofty goals is a blow to their ego. It's an insult to their self-worth—they've already told themselves they can't achieve such big things, so what makes you think you're so special? People don't like the possibility that someone who started where they did could end up so far ahead. It forces them to ask uncomfortable questions.

What am I doing wrong? Aren't I doing everything I was told?

In the United States, immigrants are twice as likely to start their own business. They haven't grown up with the same perspective on money. They weren't told: "Go to school, pile on the debt, and the system will take care of you."

In fact, many are here *precisely* because the system where they came from failed them.

Forty percent of Fortune 500 companies were founded by immigrants or the children of immigrants. They weren't bound by an entrenched social circle intent on preventing them from rising up and making a better life for themselves. They came here for opportunity, and they took it.

Don't be shamed out of your own ambitions.

YOU'LL NEVER GET RICH BY SPENDING LESS

Most Americans live paycheck to paycheck. The only advice those at the top will offer them is to live within their means and save as much as they can. In other words, to live like they're poorer than they already are so that one day they'll be able to stop working.

Many people work their entire lives for the promise of a secure retirement and never see it. Maybe they don't live long enough. Maybe something happens that dries up all of their savings. Maybe they're just terrible at managing money.

"Live within your means" is a way of telling you to shut up and stop complaining.

Yes, you shouldn't spend more money than you make, but instead of focusing on living within your means, you should focus on increasing your means.

We all have a baseline we have to spend to meet our needs. This baseline goes up as we make more money—food is a need, but we decide that we *need* better food. Clothes are a need, but when you start making more money you'll decide you *need* to replace all those shirts you've had since college.

Your "must-haves" tend to grow with your income, up to a point. Once I had a decent house in a good neighborhood, a nice car, and dinner out a couple nights a week, my expenses stopped growing. My income did not, allowing me to save more and more every month.

By focusing on increasing my means instead of living within them, my net worth grew faster than it would have by saving $10 or $100 a month. Now, saving $10, $100 or $1,000 is no big deal. I don't have to give up my morning coffee or find other places to cut back.

I'm not telling you to go wild with your spending. I'm suggesting that instead of spending hours every week trying to budget and cut corners, use that time and energy to work on your top-line income.

LEARN TO MAKE MONEY, *THEN* DO WHAT YOU LOVE

Most of us have heard the expression, "Do what you love and you'll never work a day in your life."

If they mean *do what you love and you'll never get paid for a day of work in your life*, then they're not far off.

Should you follow your passion? I thought so. After high school I decided I wanted to be a literary fiction author. I skipped college, rented a cheap apartment with a couple friends, and worked part-time so I could write.

It was awful. I had no money. The only car I could afford was a $400, twenty-year-old clunker that leaked oil everywhere. Not ideal for dates, which I couldn't afford, either. I cut my spending down to bare bones. I rarely left the house and seldom ate. I was following my passion, and hating every second of it.

I lucked out. Quite by accident, I learned how to make money by writing books. I don't mean I made money writing books—that's almost impossible. The experience of writing and rejection forced me to learn a lot of entrepreneurial skills.

If I'd done it the other way around and learned how to make money first, I would have saved myself many years of eating ramen. It's much easier to follow your dreams after you've created passive-income streams so you can focus on your passion instead of how you're going to pay the electric bill.

Here's how I learned to make money:

I wrote a book.

I couldn't get it published, so I wrote another one.

I couldn't get that one published, either.

Every rejection I got was a form letter. No one even wanted to see the manuscript.

Eventually I had four complete books and not one was published.

I looked into self-publishing. Every published author told me not to do it. If you self-publish, you won't sell more than fifty books, mostly to friends and family. They said to wait until you're good enough to be picked up by a real publishing house.

This made no sense to me. If no publishing house would read anything I'd written, I'd never be "good enough."

Most people would have given up before starting a book, telling themselves they can't do it. More would have given up while writing. The rest would have probably given up after the hundredth rejection letter.

If I had done that, I'd be a lot poorer today.

I ended up self-publishing, which meant I was completely responsible for promoting my book. I was determined to make it a success.

Online social networks were new at the time. I created a profile and started writing short stories and publishing them for free to anyone following me. I had thirty thousand bookmarks printed with the cover art from the book and asked fans of my short stories to hand them out at bookstores, coffee shops, and libraries around the country.

I taught myself pay-per-click marketing, a new trend that was gaining traction thanks to a website called Google.

I got my book on Amazon, and when it started to gain traction, I e-mailed every local reporter I could find an address for and offered to do interviews. Of course, most of them didn't care, but a few did, and a handful of articles were written about the new local fiction author.

When doing my research, every article I read about self-publishing talked about how bad it was and how it guaranteed nobody would ever read your book.

I could have complained about how artists don't get paid what they're worth. It's easier to believe that the system is set up for you to fail than it is to figure out how to use the system.

I ended up selling a couple thousand copies of my first book. Definitely not Stephen King level, but for a self-published nobody, I was proud that thousands of people paid to read my work. My girlfriend at the time couldn't figure out why I was wasting so much time when the return was so low. I understood where she was coming from. At one point I calculated that I made around 50 cents an hour while writing and promoting the book.

Looking back, I don't see it as a low-paying job. I see it as a low-paying education. I walked away with the skills to be an entrepreneur and, even better, no student debt.

I realized two things from the experience. First, if people tell you something is impossible, they're really just saying they believe it's impossible for them. Second, I was much better at marketing than I was at writing fiction. I just needed something easier to promote than a fiction novel from an unknown author.

Marketing's not something I love. I'd never choose to do it in my free time. I suppose I don't hate it.

I do love financial stability.

I love passive income.

I love that I can do whatever I'm passionate about now because I have the free time to pursue whatever activity I want.

I wrote my first book in an apartment I shared with two roommates. I had an army cot for a bed and lived on $2 a day. I'm writing this book from my second house in

Texas, a beach in Belize, an apartment in Amsterdam, the Bellagio in Las Vegas, and Disney World in Orlando.

Learn to make money first, *then* do what you love.

BE CREATIVE

You're the only person responsible for your financial future. There's just one rule, and the system doesn't care about you.

Use your brain. It's the best tool you've got. Get creative and follow the money.

The idea of cash-back credit cards have intrigued me since they started showing up several years ago. Previously, you could get credit cards that gave you rewards like airline miles, but for the first time, credit card companies were giving people cash to use their cards.

Anytime people are giving out free money, you should pay attention.

I found a card that gave me 5 percent back on gas purchases. When gas was $4 a gallon, the credit card company paid me $3 every time I filled up my tank.

There are cards that pay up to 6 percent back on every dollar you spend at a grocery store. For the average American family of four, that's almost $60 a month in cash back.

It's free money, and you don't have to mess around with coupons. It's automatic.

Of course, they're hoping you'll miss a payment and so they can make all of that money back, but even if you don't, they still come out ahead because every store has to pay the credit card company for processing transactions.

Now it's not a ton of money, but depending on your cards and your spending habits, you could squeeze $100 a month out of the credit card companies.

That's money you wouldn't have had otherwise. Go ahead and invest it. A hundred bucks every month for forty years in a tax-deferred mutual fund can grow to over a million dollars by the time you retire. It's much easier to give up $100 a month when it wasn't yours to begin with.

Now as I've said, I'm not one for waiting until retirement to be wealthy.

I started looking for ways to make more free money from the credit card companies. Ideally, I wanted something roughly equivalent to a salary, paid by Visa and American Express.

As far as I could tell, the only way to make that happen was to use OPM.

WHAT IS OPM?

Pronounced like "opium," OPM is short for "other people's money." Like the drug, it's powerful and addictive stuff. It can make you rich, or it can keep you in debt your whole life.

When you take out a mortgage to buy a house, you're using other people's money. When you start a business and get investors, you're using other people's money. If you're not already rich, one of the fastest ways to become rich is by using other people's money.

So what does OPM have to do with credit cards?

I learned of the concept of using OPM to make money when I was working at a company that sold electronics. The company spent a ton of money on advertising, but it wasn't getting the return on investment needed to keep buying the expensive ads.

That's when they went to the manufacturers of the electronics. They showed the manufacturer exactly how many extra units they were selling because of the ads. After impressing the manufacturer with how much extra business the ads were generating, they broke the news that they'd be unable to continue running the ads because they were too expensive.

The manufacturer agreed to step up and foot half the bill. With the marketing cost cut in half, the company was able to run even more ads and sold millions of units.

It was amazing to me to see the company's bottom line go from negative to hundreds of thousands of dollars in the black in a week thanks to a single deal. They didn't change any processes or business practices. They just started using other people's money.

I wanted to try my hand at it.

As I mentioned, the company I was working for was spending a ton of money on advertisements. I went through all the accounts and found roughly $50 million a year that could be put on a credit card but was currently being paid by invoice.

I went to my boss with a proposal. He could stop paying my salary tomorrow. I would work for free.

In return, he'd let me put the expenses on my cash-back credit card. The company would reimburse me, and I'd keep all the rewards from the credit card company.

He didn't go for it. At least, he didn't let me use my card. I wouldn't be surprised if someone higher up ended up with a few million airline miles the next year.

While this attempt ended in failure, it didn't cost me anything. I was still anxious to try out the idea when I started my company a few years later. One of the first things I did when I went off on my own was to get a couple cash-back cards and use them to pay for almost all of my expenses.

Here's how I looked at it: If a company is operating at a 10 percent net margin, getting just 2 percent back on all their expenditures would boost their profits by 20 percent. If you raised the profits of any company by 20 percent overnight, you'd be a hero.

The cash back didn't amount to much at first, but once the business got off the ground, I was spending about $3 to $4 million a year and putting most of it on credit cards.

Two percent cash back from $4 million is $80,000. That's completely free money I wouldn't have if I were paying those same bills by check. Even if my company was only breaking even, I'd still be able to pay myself a decent salary every year.

Fortunately, the business was making enough money to pay me even without the extra money from the credit card companies. Remember how I said to invest that $100 a month from your cash-back card? If I take half of that $80,000 every year and put it in a solid mutual fund, it'll be worth more than $20 million by the time I hit sixty-five. Visa and American Express are effectively giving me a multimillion dollar pension, and I don't even work for them.

I don't put all of my spending on a cash-back card, though. Some of it goes on a card that gives me airline miles so I can travel for free whenever I want. Why wait until you're sixty-five to have fun?

Be smart and creative with money, or you'll be paying 20 percent interest on your credit debt and funding my retirement.

DON'T PLAY THE LOTTERY

Don't go broke trying to get rich.

Creating value isn't always fun. Even though creating value isn't difficult once you figure it out, it's easier to sell people on scams about easy money. So many of these scams exist that it's hard to find good information on building wealth.

For instance, I could recommend that everyone take their life savings to Las Vegas, find a roulette wheel, and bet on the number fourteen. I'd have a lot of success stories. A lot of people would make a fortune.

Many more would lose their life savings. Whose testimonials do you think I'd publish on my website?

Many get-rich-quick schemes aren't much different. For every positive testimonial you read, there are thousands of people with stories of heartache and loss.

Some scammers will sell you on a "unique" stock trading system. Through sheer luck, some of their students will do extremely well and others will lose their homes. You won't see stories on their websites from people who lost everything.

If you're investing your savings, just find a low-fee mutual fund tied to the S&P 500. The stock market is a way for rich people to get richer. If you're Warren Buffet, you can pick stocks. You are not Warren Buffet. Yes, it's possible to start with a small amount of money and make millions, just like it's possible to spend $5 on a lottery ticket and hit the jackpot.

The stock market draws people the same way the lottery does. I've often heard the lottery called "The Math Tax." The idea is that people who play the lottery don't realize what a bad investment it is because they're excited by the potential payout. Instead of thinking about the odds, they start daydreaming about the life they'll have when they win. They'll spend money they need on a chance at money they'll never win. I think most lottery players know this, which is why I don't consider the lottery a tax on people who aren't good at math. I consider the lottery a tax on hope.

People fall for get-rich-quick scams for the same reason. They're buying hope, and for many people, that's their only plan for the future. They hope they'll have a great idea for a business. They hope a rich, unknown relative will die and leave them a fortune. Maybe they'll get a hot stock tip, bet everything, and become a billionaire. They want desperately to be rich, but all they do is hope.

Does that describe you? What have you done to get rich? Have you spent your life up until now hoping?

Luck isn't going to come along and make you wealthy. Sure, it's happened to a few people, but you're not one of them. If the odds of getting a fortune through sheer luck are so miniscule, how many lifetimes are you going to have to wait before it happens to you?

I don't know the answer, but I do know you only get one. Don't waste it playing the lottery. Have a plan, and work to fix the odds in your favor.

DON'T CHEAT

"Behind every great fortune there is a crime."
—Honoré de Balzac

It's certainly true that a lot of people have taken shortcuts on the way to wealth, whether unethically or illegally. It's certainly not true that every wealthy person only got that way by cheating. You shouldn't, either, for the same reason you shouldn't play the lottery. You only live once. Bernie Madoff made billions by defrauding others. He will die alone in a jail cell.

You might think you're smarter than everyone else and can rip people off without getting caught. Maybe you can, for a while. In chapter eight, I'll detail a few people who thought the same way whose lives are now ruined.

Eventually it'll come back to bite you, and in the meantime, you'll spend your life waiting for it to happen. The biggest reason to become wealthy is so you can enjoy life.

If you're always waiting for the cops to show up at your door, you're not enjoying life.

Your one life is too important to leave to chance.

CHAPTER 4

A ROUGH START

I was ten years old when the uniformed Fairfax County sheriff knocked on our door. Inside, the house was bare except for a few boxes, some toys left out for my three siblings and me, and a picnic blanket on the living room floor. We had ordered a pizza the night before, and the six of us ate our last meal together in our family home.

My mom opened the door. The sheriff looked pained and embarrassed. "Please," he said, "don't make me kick you out."

My mom knew he was just doing his job, and it was time for us to leave. It had only been two years since my parents had achieved their dream of owning their own home—a beautiful place in their childhood hometown across from the local middle school. There was a big yard for my brothers, my sister, and me to play in surrounded by a white picket fence covered in honeysuckle and morning glories. It was so idyllic that a picture of our fence with the flowers in full bloom currently graced the cover of our town's official 1992 calendar, a copy of which sat neatly packed away in one of the boxes inside.

"It's okay," my mom said. "We're going now."

"I'm sorry," said the sheriff.

He meant it, too. This wasn't the first time he'd met my parents. He was a regular at Margarita's, the restaurant my father had started more than a decade earlier. At least, the sheriff *had* been a regular.

In 1980 my father, twenty years old at the time, opened a restaurant with his father and named it after my grandmother. My father built the interior by hand, and by the time I was born a year later, the restaurant had taken its final form—stucco walls covered in velvet bullfighters, colorful serapes, black-and-white photos of Pancho Villa and old Mexican towns, and the all-you-can-eat taco bar in the center.

I started working there as a busboy at seven years old. It was my own choice, and the truth is, I enjoyed it—not the running around refilling drinks or cleaning off dirty tables part, but the self-sufficiency that came from having a job. I enjoyed making money. I could pull in $30 a night—which to a seven-year-old in 1988 was a small fortune.

My older brother also worked at the restaurant. He spent his extra money on clothes, which I thought was frivolous. I spent my money on candy and video games. My dad tried to convince me to invest in mutual funds and explained how the money could grow and even double over time, but after hearing that I'd have to leave the money untouched for years, I decided against it.

My parents put us kids to work at home, too. My dad would regularly get a list of all the new families that had moved into the area recently, and he'd have us stuff envelopes to mail to them. Inside was a letter welcoming them to town, along with a coupon and an invitation to try our restaurant.

On the weekends, a mariachi singer named Jesus would come to the restaurant and perform on a small stage. One song he sang stuck out in my mind. The chorus had him repeating "*que bueno*" over and over.

Curious, I went to my grandmother and asked, "What does '*que bueno*' mean?"

"The song is about things being so good," she said.

Around the turn of the decade, I noticed a change at the restaurant. Jesus stopped showing up on the weekends. At home I could hear my parents arguing after we went to bed.

A recession hit in the middle of 1990. Though I'd just turned nine, I can still remember the newspaper headlines from the time and the bleak picture they were painting. I didn't give it much thought because I had a more immediate concern—an economic crises of my own.

Something happened while I approached my first double-digit birthday. My tips were shrinking. I was growing into a preteen body and was decidedly less cute. It was really cutting into my take-home pay.

There were, of course, bigger issues. In the end, Margarita's went under and took our family's financial future with it.

My father and I were the last two to leave the restaurant the night it closed for good. It was early December 1991. I stood beside him while he placed the key in the lock and turned it for the last time. It was after midnight, and the strip mall that had been home to Margarita's for more than a decade was deserted.

"It's the end of a chapter," he said to me. I could hear his voice shaking.

He knelt down and forced a smile. "Now we get to turn the page and see what God has in store next."

He put his arms around me. I could feel the months of stress, the fear of what would come next, and his own need to make sure his family was always taken care of all hit him at once. It's the most vivid memory I have of my childhood and a moment that continues to have a huge impact on my life.

The collapse of my father's business left my parents with no savings, poor credit, a mountain of debt, and no source of income. Neither of them had a college degree. Though the recent recession was technically over, unemployment was still rising, and our family's prospects were not looking good.

Then came the knock on the door that spring. The bank had foreclosed on the house, and we had to leave.

We were fortunate enough to have family in the area that could take us in. We moved in with my mom's parents, taking over a couple rooms upstairs. Not wanting to be a burden, my mom made sure to lay down the ground rules: Stay upstairs. No going downstairs without asking Grandma. It was only temporary, they told us. In a month, two at most, we'd have our own place.

It was years before we moved out on our own again. Being poor sucks. It feels like a prison and there's no way out. The remainder of my childhood was a struggle to make ends meet, and my parents were in no position to help me financially when I turned eighteen and had to make it on my own.

WHY "GET RICH" BOOKS SUCK

I didn't want to end up like my parents, but things didn't look promising. I had no money for college. Taking out huge student loans seemed like a bad idea, and I was never a very good student anyway. Obviously, my parents couldn't help.

While all my friends went to college, I spent my early adulthood working low-wage jobs with no career path. Like my parents, I was just trying to survive.

I wanted to learn how to get rich and stay rich, so I spent a lot of time reading books about money.

My dad taught me a fun game when I was a kid called *Spot the Scam*. Whenever a piece of junk mail showed up at our house, he'd hand it to me and it was my job to figure out how the junk mail sender was trying to scam us. I was young, but I caught on the weasel-wording pretty quick.

"You may have already won!" the letter might say.

"It means we didn't win," I'd tell my dad, who then nodded in approval.

"You're preapproved!" said another.

"It means some guy preapproved us to get the letter. If we were approved, it would say we were approved."

This game was still in the back of my head as I read many of the more popular books about making money. I had one nagging thought as I turned the pages:

A lot of people have read these books, and most of them still aren't rich.

Why was that? What was stopping the people reading these books from becoming wealthy?

The more I read, the clearer the problem became. A lot of these books promoted investing, which is a great idea under the right circumstances. Some books talked about how to buy real estate and rent it out for profit.

I was making $8 an hour. What four-unit condo building was I going to buy on $8 an hour?

Others mentioned long-term investments in the stock market. *It's all so easy*, these experts would say. *If you invest $100,000 at an 8 percent annual return, you'll have a million dollars in roughly thirty years.*

Can you wait thirty years? Do you have $100,000? I know I didn't.

Occasionally one of these books about making money would mention immediate returns. The author would talk about a big deal they managed to close that let them turn an investment of a few million dollars into many more millions of dollars.

How does that help anyone?

Mostly, though, the books I read just talked about ways to cut back and save money. The authors were convinced that the only reason people were poor was because they spent too much money, and the only path to wealth was extreme frugality.

When I was a teenager, my parents had already cut their expenses as much as possible. We didn't even have a home. We spent years living with relatives. How could my parents have saved their way out of that situation?

How could two people making just over minimum wage with four kids and $100,000 in debt (in today's money) become rich by saving money? They were maxing out credit cards just to keep us fed.

They couldn't, because that advice is dumb.

If you've tried and failed to get wealthy by saving money, you're not alone.

YOU CAN'T SAVE YOUR WAY TO WEALTH

Many financial experts say that if you're poor, you can save your way to wealth.

They are wrong, and you can't.

When I was poor and read things like, "Save $100 every month and you'll have a million dollars by the time you're sixty-five!" I'd get angry.

I don't need a million dollars when I'm sixty-five, I need $100 now!

I'd feel ripped off.

I couldn't save $100 a month. I couldn't save $10 a month.

"It's simple," they tell you. "Keep saving money and you'll be rich when you retire!"

The life expectancy for a male born when I was is seventy. So if I spent the first sixty-five years of my life on a really tight budget, I could have a full five years of easy living.

That's crap.

The most insulting advice went something like this:

"Drink one less $4 latte a day, invest that $4 and you'll be rich!"

How many $4 lattes do these guys think poor people are drinking every day?

It's amazing to me how many authors have been able to make a living telling people that the answer to their money problems is to stop spending money. It's lazy, but it's the best these guys have to offer. Most of it is regurgitated from wealth advisers who only make money by convincing others that they know how to make money. None of them know how to significantly speed up the process of wealth creation because they've never actually done it.

Even a mentor who's hit it big would struggle to point you in the right direction. What's Mark Zuckerberg going to tell you? He's a smart guy, but what advice is he going to give you that will make you rich? Make the next Facebook?

How helpful is that?

The idea of saving your way to wealth is pushed by a lot of financial advisors, because telling you to save money is easy. Teaching you how to actually build wealth in a reasonable amount of time is a lot harder.

Don't get me wrong. Saving is great, and it's an important tool, but you'll have to do more than put away a few bucks a month to be rich anytime soon.

If you wrote a self-help book called *How To Be a Better Person Forty Years From Now*, would anyone buy it?

What about *How To Be More Spiritual. Not Now but, Like, Just Before You Die*.

Or

Lose that Extra Belly Fat in Just 5,000 Workout Sessions!

If people really believed they had to diet their whole lives just so they could start losing weight in their sixties, do you think anyone would ever diet?

I know I wouldn't.

So why do we all listen to the advice that we need to live beneath our means our whole lives for a moderate payout at the end?

You probably already know this, but it doesn't work. When you're poor, you can't save money. All of it goes to meeting your basic needs.

You cannot save your way out of poverty.

If you are poor, you cannot save your way to wealth.

I know this contradicts almost everything you've heard about money, so let's run the numbers real quick.

Let's assume you work a job with mediocre pay and you do very little over the course of your life to increase your income. If you start saving when you're twenty-five and put it all in solid investments, it's possible you'll have a million dollars in the bank by the time you're sixty-five.

Before you celebrate, keep in mind that you've spent the majority of your life scraping by to make ends meet. Also, in forty years, a million dollars will be worth around $200,000 to $250,000 of today's money due to inflation. Yes, it's nice to have a quarter million dollars in a bank account, but you won't be buying a Ferrari anytime soon. You'll have to make that $250,000 last the rest of your life.

That's not a path to wealth. It's a guarantee that you'll spend the rest of your life worrying about money.

That's assuming you're even able to put aside money. Let's be honest. If saving money is hard, you won't do it. It's the same with investing. Given a choice between money today or more money thirty years from now, people will almost always choose money today. We're human, and most of us can't help it.

So how can anyone break the cycle of poverty?

There's only one solution, and it's a paradox.

The first step to being rich is to not be poor.

I know that sounds so simple as to be insulting, but it's something every poor person needs to think about.

As long as you are not making a lot of money, it is impossible to save a lot of money.

The trick to saving money is to have a lot of it to save.

Saving money on a meager income is very hard to do. Saving money when you're making a lot of it is much easier.

We'll get into the specifics, but first I want you to stop focusing on only one part of the equation. Think about all the time you've spent coming up with ways to save money. How much money do you think you've saved?

What if you'd spent all that time coming up with ways to make more money?

If you're trying to get rich by saving money, your choice will only ever be to spend more or save more. If you instead shift your focus to the other half of the equation, you can spend more *and* save more.

Perhaps you've heard of the expression "penny wise and pound foolish." It refers to people who spend so much time trying to get the little things right that they mess up the important stuff. If you're always looking for ways to save a few cents but haven't done anything proactive to increase your income, you are penny wise and pound foolish.

It's important to be smart about the money you already have, but all the time you spend thinking up ways to save a dollar are better spent coming up with ways to earn ten. The goal is to be rich, not less poor.

I'm not against saving. I'm against spending more time trying to save a buck than figuring out how to make several bucks.

It is much easier to make an extra $1,000 a month than to save an extra $1,000 a month.

If you take one thing away from this book, it should be this:

Don't live beneath your means. Increase your means.

MONEY THAT'S NEVER SPENT IS WORTHLESS

People want to be rich so they can buy the things they want, yet they're told that to become rich, they have to not buy the things they want. It's no wonder this frugality-first mentality causes people to get discouraged.

What's the point of being rich if you live like you're poor?

You'll likely never see most of the money you make in your lifetime. It will exist only as 1's and 0's on a computer at a bank. If you live your whole life like you have no money, it's no different than actually having no money.

Being rich is pointless if you don't use the wealth to improve your life.

A lot of people have read the book *The Millionaire Next Door*. Its author divides people into two groups, Under Accumulators of Wealth (UAWs) and Prodigious Accumulators of Wealth (PAWs). Essentially, the author scores people on the percentage of their income they are able to save. If you make $40,000 a year and have $500,000 in the bank, you're better at accumulating wealth than someone your same age making $500,000 a year with $2 million in the bank.

This is a bunch of crap.

Wealth isn't graded on a curve. What matters is the final number. You don't get points for doing less with less. We've become so obsessed with the saving side of the equation that income is ignored like it's an unchangeable number. Why do so many people believe they only have control over what they spend?

The person with $2 million in the bank is wealthier and doing much better financially than the person with a quarter of that.

If you double your income, even if you also double your spending, you're still accumulating wealth faster and enjoying a richer lifestyle than you were before you increased your income.

The author makes the argument that the person who has saved a higher multiplier of their annual income is better able to keep up their lifestyle if something happens to their income stream. All that argument really means is that you need practice at being poor so you're more comfortable with being poor.

The popularity of the logic behind *The Millionaire Next Door* demonstrates a problem with our money mind-set. We look at the income and savings equation and think we can only control one side. For some reason, we blindly accept the income we're assigned, and the game is all about how much of it we're able to save.

A person with a meager income who spends fifty years working for other people and manages to save a relatively large nest egg that lets him live like the middle class for a few years in retirement did not live a financially wealthy life.

81

Sure, it beats having a meager income, no savings, and having to depend on younger relatives to take care of you in your old age, but that's setting the bar pretty low.

Let's take a look at someone on the other end of the spectrum. He's a fictional character, but were he real, he'd definitely be in the Prodigious Accumulator of Wealth group.

His name is Ebenezer Scrooge, of *Christmas Carol* fame.

After getting a good education, Scrooge enters the world of business. He is very smart with his money and doesn't waste it on frivolities like partying with his friends or expensive displays of wealth. He saves money by not heating his house (or his business) any more than absolutely necessary. At night, he only keeps the lights on in one room at a time.

Scrooge invests in real estate. He can support himself on passive income. He also made the brilliant financial decision not to have any children. Families cost a lot of money.

Scrooge lives far below his means. In many ways, he lives as if he's a poorer man than Bob Cratchit, his underpaid assistant. As a result, Scrooge has saved a substantial fortune. He's a legendary accumulator of wealth and can keep up his lifestyle indefinitely, or at least until a bunch of ghosts come and ruin everything.

Is Scrooge the hero we should be looking up to?

Would the story have had a happy ending if Scrooge lived the rest of his life as a PAW and died with an enormous and unused fortune?

Of course not. In fact, seeing that future version of his life is the final vision that scares Scrooge into becoming a better person.

The happy ending comes when Scrooge uses his wealth to enjoy life and help others.

I don't want to be like pre-Christmas Scrooge. What's the point of having wealth that you don't use? I'll never understand the mind-set of people who think being rich means living like you're poor your whole life while a number on a bank computer slowly grows.

A ROAD MAP

Yes, it's possible to become rich without hoarding every dollar and living like a miser.
Most adults are only three steps away from being wealthy and living life on their own terms. Some people never complete these three simple steps in their lifetime, yet others are able to achieve them in a few years or less.

I've mentioned the third step already. It's the one people giving financial advice like to jump ahead to because it's the most fun, but it's useless until you've gone through the first two steps.

These steps are obvious, and you probably already know them. Yet so many people are stuck in dead-end jobs wondering why their financial situation isn't what they'd hoped for, and it's because they forgot the three simple steps to becoming wealthy:

Stop the (financial) bleeding.
Increase your income.

83

Make your money

Before you say "d
down. This is your road m

Stop the bleeding
Increase your inc
Make your mone

Did you write it d
of paper somewhere you
first thing you should do when you wake up is to ask yourself which of those three steps you're going to work on. Get into the habit of thinking about your finances before they become an issue, not when you have a fiscal emergency and it's time to hit the panic button.

There's a passage in Sun Tzu's *The Art of War* that I often reference. Sun Tzu was a Chinese general who lived more than two thousand years ago. Although his advice was intended for military strategists on ancient battlefields, *The Art of War* is actually one of the best books on business you can read.

The quote in the book I always come back to is:

"Victorious warriors win first and then go to war, while defeated warriors go to war first and then seek to win."

In other words, battles are won or lost before they're fought, because the difference between winning and losing is preparation.

Most people only think about money when they have to. When disaster strikes is not the time to wish you had an extra $10,000. Think about how you're going to

before you need it so that it's
strikes.

es to all aspects of life. Don't wait until
eone you find attractive to start wishing
more time at the gym. Don't wait until you get
to start looking for a better job. When someone is
cally attacking you, it's the wrong time to think about
arning some form of self-defense.

Too many of us only think about money when
there's an emergency or we've just read about someone
winning the lottery.

There's a big part of our culture that looks down
on talking about or even thinking too much about money.
Many people have significant others who shun the
discussion of money (but those same partners are the
first to complain when there's a financial problem). If you
really want to be wealthy, you're going to have to ignore a
lot of people who are upset by your financial focus.

Stop the bleeding.
Increase your income.
Make your money work for you.

Most financial advice fails because it only focuses
on step one or step three. The primary purpose of this
book is to fill the gap, but we have to make sure your
bases are covered so you can start and finish strong on
your journey to wealth.

STOP THE BLEEDING

Having all the money in the world won't make a difference if you can't hold on to it. We need to make sure you're getting into the right habits.

If you have money issues, chances are you fall into one of three categories I'm about to address. These are:

Debtors
Coasters
Consumers

Now don't take these labels too literally. People in each of these groups likely have debt and buy things (consume), but it's a good way to segment people based on income and where they need the most help.

Each situation requires a different set of tools.

The problem with too much of the current money advice available is that it tells Debtors things that Consumers need to do or vice versa. The advice is solid if aimed at the correct group but disastrous for someone in a different financial position.

All three groups have money issues, but if you told someone with no job and no cash (Debtor) to invest in rental properties, you'd be wasting their time. Mutual funds? Roth IRAs? Blue chip stocks? If you're in the Debtor group, you know how ridiculous that advice sounds.

DEBTORS

Just having debt does not get you into this group. People at all income levels have debt, but the people in this group are being crushed by it.

Depending on who you believe, between 20 and 50 percent of Americans have a negative net worth. They owe more in debt than they own.

People in the Debtor group are poor. Including debt, they actually have less than no money. You may have a picture in your head of who might fall into this group, but you'd probably be surprised. There are many smart, well-educated people in the Debtor group, but, unfortunately, our school system taught them very little about making money. Ironically, Debtors owe a lot of their debt to that same school system.

In recent years, the United States has seen huge growth in the amount of outstanding student loan debt. Not only has the price of college risen astronomically, but much of the cost is being financed by loans. A hundred thousand dollars for school could cost a quarter million dollars or more by the time it's paid off. Many recent graduates are facing decades of negative net worth.

If you're in high school, do your research and make sure the college degree you want is really worth the price you'll pay for it. For me, it wasn't. I skipped college and saved myself a small fortune. It's the main reason that, although I've been very poor, I've never had a negative net worth. The decision to skip college is not for everyone and not a decision to be made lightly, but the one-size-fits-all plan of going to college no matter the cost is not always the best path.

Many millennials left college with not only tens or hundreds of thousands of dollars in student loan debt, but also managed to rack up tons of credit card debt. This isn't too surprising—it's hard to find time to work while you're earning a degree, and credit card companies offer a way to pay your bills in the meantime.

It's the start of a lifetime pattern. You don't have enough cash to pay all your bills because of the interest you're paying on your debts, so now you have to borrow more. This is a common problem—the average US household has around $16,000 of credit card debt. That is insane. That means the average household is paying $2,400 annually just in debt financing. If you have a poor credit score, you're paying even more.

Some people are in so much debt that they can't pay their bills on time and turn to payday loans. These loans have astronomical interest rates, but many Debtors see them as their only solution.

It's not a solution. It just makes the problem worse the next month. Many payday loan shops charge around $15 for a $100 loan that must be paid back in two weeks. That works out to a 400 percent APR—meaning that borrowing and paying back $1,000 every two weeks will cost you $4,000 every year.

Many lenders charge even more. It's a downward spiral. If you take out a payday loan, you'll have even less money when you get your next paycheck and you'll need to take out more and more loans.

Even though you feel poor, you're actually making a lot of money—for other people. Debtors are a cash cow.

If you're in this situation, you're in good company. We have this problem as a country, as well. After many years of not balancing its budget, the US government owes nearly $20 trillion. The cost to finance that debt every year is in the hundreds of billions. That's a lot of tax dollars we have to chip in because of old debt.

There is one positive side to having a lot of personal debt. Your investment options are very straightforward, and they have a great guaranteed return on investment.

If you're poor and wondering how you're supposed to invest in real estate, the answer is you're not.

You can stop reading about exciting new investments. You don't have to worry about getting a hot stock tip. Don't waste your time thinking about day-trading. Don't try it, either. You'll just end up in more debt.

If you have high-interest debt, the best investment you can make is paying off what you owe.

Let's take a look at some other traditional investments. U.S treasury bonds are considered the closest thing to a sure bet in the world. What that means is, while there's always a chance you'll lose 100 percent of what you invest, bonds are considered a safer investment and US treasury bonds are at the top of the list.

Unfortunately, the current annual return is less than 3 percent. So let's say you've got $100 to invest and don't know where to put it. If you invest that $100 in treasury bonds, four years from now you'll have about $108.

If you have $100 in credit card debt with a 19 percent interest rate and don't pay it off, in four years you'll owe $200.

Investing in a "sure thing" gets you $8, but you've actually lost $92 by not paying off your debt. If you had paid off the debt instead, you'd have saved yourself $100

89

in interest charges. That's a 100 percent return on investment. I promise you'll never find another investment that is guaranteed to double your money every four years.

Even if you consider other, riskier investments like the stock market that average around 10 percent in returns each year, you're still better off paying down your high-interest debt.

When it comes to credit cards, there are really only two options:

Pay off your entire balance every month.
Don't have credit cards.

A lot of Debtors argue that they need their credit cards. I understand—my parents were poor for many years, and sometimes we would have gone hungry if they hadn't used their credit card. It just made it even harder the next month when, instead of buying groceries, my parents had to pay the interest on the credit card bill. In the end, the credit card company made more off the groceries than the grocery store did.

Instead of solving the problem, high-interest debt only makes it worse.

The other argument I've heard from Debtors about needing a credit card is that it builds your credit score. Unfortunately, if you can't make your payments, not only are you losing money to interest but you're actually destroying your credit score.

If you can't pay it off every month, don't have a credit card. Sure, it will be hard at first. Being poor sucks. If it were easy to get out of poverty, there'd be no poor people in the world.

Some people are too far down in the hole. If you are so deep in debt you can't see any way out, there are a few extreme options available.

Like my parents, you could declare bankruptcy. This is the nuclear option and should only be considered when all other options have been exhausted. There are two types of personal bankruptcy, one that allows you to restructure your payments to your creditors, and another type that wipes out most personal debt.

Keep in mind, bankruptcy can stay on your credit record for up to a decade. However, if you've reached this point, your credit score may be damaged enough that the addition of bankruptcy won't affect it as severely.

Don't forget, if someone cosigned for your debt they're likely still on the hook to pay it off. It's possible you'll damage relationships that are important to you. Make sure you understand all the consequences before going down this path.

A less extreme option is to use a debt-reduction service, but there are consequences to this as well. Debt-reduction services negotiate with creditors on your behalf. It's possible to get your total debt negotiated down by 50 percent or more. If a creditor is offered the choice of getting 50 cents or 0 cents for each dollar of debt, they'll often agree to 50 cents. The debt-reduction service will then charge you a percentage of the savings.

Like bankruptcy, this is another avenue not to go down until you've done your research. It can wreak havoc on your credit score and have other serious consequences.

If you're in this position, check out my website. I'll have more resources available for you there so you can explore your options.

If you've reached a financial bottom, you're probably feeling a lot of pressure to start clipping coupons and cutting back on any spending that isn't absolutely essential. That's not a bad idea, but when you're poor, there's only so much to cut.

I've been there and done that, and in the long run, just cutting back won't fix the problem. Your effort is better spent figuring out how to increase your income.

COASTERS

Like most Americans, this group lives paycheck to paycheck. They're better off than the Debtors, but not by much. They've got some cash in their bank account, but not nearly enough to cover any extended period of unemployment.

Usually they're comfortable (though not happy) with their current job. They'll often daydream about a better life, better car, nicer house, but haven't a clue how to actually get it, so they put their wishes on the back burner and go back to work. It's not what they imagined they'd be doing after school, but it pays the bills.

Besides, there's more to life than money, right?

That's what most people think, until they need money.

People in this group have a decent income, maybe some student loans and a couple credit cards, but they aren't in crippling debt.

This group's biggest problem is motivation.

It's easy to come home after working all day and plop down on the couch. Financially things are "okay," so there's no harm in watching some TV or working on a hobby. This continues day after day.

It's easy to forget that the dreams you had for your life are becoming less and less likely with every year spent scraping by.

People in this group are able to save some money if they put in the effort. They're the ones who can set aside a chunk of their income, live like they're poorer than they are for a few decades, and come out with a decent nest egg for retirement. That's nice, if you're into that sort of thing. I'm not.

If you're in this group and that's not your sort of thing, either, keep reading.

CONSUMERS

Ever see a $400 pair of jeans and wonder, *Who pays that much for this stuff?* This group does.

Consumers have hit their stride in their career. They've bought their dream home, put a pool in the backyard, and parked a boat in the driveway. Even though they make a lot of money, their savings haven't grown as much as they'd expect. Where's all the money going?

People in the consumer group have good jobs, make good money, and assume that they'll keep on making good money for the rest of their working lives. Their expenses grew with their income and never stopped. They moved to a nice neighborhood with other rich people and convinced themselves they needed the same toys.

I'm all for living the good life and enjoying what you've earned, but I also wouldn't want to keep going to work if I could avoid it. Every new sports car is an investment squandered and a missed chance at building passive income.

This group doesn't have a motivation problem. They just haven't learned the most important lesson of being wealthy: just because you can afford anything you want doesn't mean you can afford *everything* you want. Not learning this lesson is the main reason why most lottery winners are broke within a few years.

Still, this group is in a great situation. They're the one group that can get rich in a reasonable amount of time while still enjoying a fantastic quality of life.

Compared to Debtors, saving and investing their way to wealth is relatively easy. The reason they can save their way to wealth isn't because they're more frugal than Debtors. Debtors are probably the most frugal people there are. Consumers are able to save their way to wealth because of their income.

A Debtor can't buy an investment property. They have a hard enough time paying rent. However, instead of buying the biggest house they can afford, a Consumer can scale back their purchase a bit and have enough left over to pick up a rental property.

I've got a lot of high-income neighbors. Most of them have great jobs and decided it was time to buy a million-dollar house. Had they been looking to build passive income, they'd have been better served by buying a home of the same size a couple miles farther away from the city for half of what they paid to live here. They could then buy a second house to rent out.

Since the rent should cover the mortgage and repairs on the second house, they'd only have half their current monthly housing expenses. When the mortgage on the second house is paid off (probably around the time they retire), they'll have a free house paid for by decades of rent.

That's why I decided not to sell my home whenever I move. I look for a nice house I can afford without freeing up cash from investments. Then I rent out the old house. When it's time for me to fully stop working, I'll have a trail of free houses behind me to fund my retirement.

I don't pay off the mortgages because they're between 3 percent and 5 percent. As long as I can find investments that pay more than 5 percent annually, I make more money by keeping the mortgage debt.

I don't feel like I'm going without anything. I still have my coffee every morning, and I travel every few weeks. That's the difference between trying to save when you're poor and investing once you've got a solid income.

INCREASE YOUR INCOME

You'll notice I don't spend a lot of time talking about ways to cut back and stop spending more than you make. There's a good reason for that, because there's one simple answer for most money problems:

$200,000 in student loans? *Make more money.*
Bankrupt? *Make more money.*

95

Can't afford a house? *Make more money.*

    I had to learn a very important lesson about investing before becoming wealthy. I once thought that the poor (like myself, at the time) had nothing to invest. That's not true.

    The rich can invest money. The poor can invest time.

    If you're poor, you should be investing your time into finding ways to increase your income. Keep in mind that while saving money and practicing frugality are seen as virtuous and intelligent, focusing on getting more money is often viewed as immoral and greedy. This is completely hypocritical—after all, why do people go to college and work to get ahead if not to make more money? Learn to ignore negativity. Devote less time to cutting back and more to growing.

DON'T WAIT

While I took issue with a lot of what I read in books about money, there was one very important kernel of truth. The secret to building wealth is starting early.

    That's why it's so important you stop worrying about how to save that $10 a month and start thinking about ways to make more money so you can save $200, $500, or $1,000 without giving anything up.

    Sure, if you're maxing out your credit cards every month, then cutting back is a good place to start, but for most people the answer to their financial issues is creating more income.

Of the three groups of people with money problems, only the Consumers are able to save their way to wealth in a reasonable amount of time, and that's solely because of their income. So let's stop talking about saving money and work on increasing your take-home pay.

CHAPTER 5

BUILD YOUR RESUME—HOW TO MAKE MONEY WORKING FOR OTHER PEOPLE

I looked around for somewhere to set my drink. I was about to ask the woman next to me to hold it before I saw that her hands were full. She was holding an enormous albino python.

For the second time in my life, a uniformed police officer was kicking me out of a house. This time the officer was on horseback, and the horse seemed a bit unnerved by the white tiger staring at it from a few feet away.

A line of go-go dancers streamed out of the house between me and the cop. It was the distraction I needed to go back inside. It was going to take the cops awhile to kick everyone out of the mansion, and I didn't want to leave yet. I walked past the shallow indoor pool, the water bubbling from the falling rain coming from the showerheads mounted in the ceiling. As I passed the bookshelf hiding the secret passage to the hidden wine cellar, I wondered if the poker game was going to be broken up or if it was safe from the cops down there.

I went out the back door to the pool where the DJ was still playing loud music and couples were hooking up in the grotto behind the waterfall.

This is crazy, I thought, downing the rest of my drink and setting it on the counter of the outdoor bar. *I'm here for work. I'm getting paid for this.*

LEAVE YOUR COMFORT ZONE

Why am I not making more money? I work hard. I'm a good person.

I meet a lot of people with this mentality. It's hard to believe that the world isn't going to reward us for doing our part: working hard and being a decent human being. Unfortunately, neither is a guarantee that you'll be wealthy.

For most jobs, your pay is based on two factors. The first is your perceived value add—how much the company expects to make from your work. The second factor is how hard it would be to replace you.

For instance, if you work in human resources, it's hard to put an exact dollar amount on the value you provide to a company. An employer will likely offer you a salary relative to what other companies are paying for similar positions. It's the same for most positions that don't directly affect a company's bottom line.

These jobs all have little to no monetary accountability. If you want a career with less pressure, one that lets you eke out a living without constantly being evaluated based on the revenue you're generating, then these are the kind of jobs you want.

It's almost impossible to become wealthy
way. The only people who do well financially in the
are the ones who make themselves hard to replace.
fast-food employee walks out in the middle of their shi
it's not going to affect the business very much. If an
airline pilot doesn't show up for work, there's going to be
a problem.

The value of a person in a sales position is very
easy to quantify. That's why poor salesmen make very
little money and good salesmen make tons of money.
You can't skate by—if you slack, you don't get paid. If
you hustle, you make lots of money.

Get in a position where your value is easy to
quantify, then work as hard as you can to show your
value.

A lot of people think this is wrong. They shouldn't
have to change their line of work, their career, or
abandon their passion just to get ahead.

You can try to change society. If that's your goal,
then good luck, but get used to being poor in the
meantime. The other option is to work toward changing
your individual circumstances. I don't need to tell you
which one is easier.

EDUCATION

Is a college degree worth it?

This is by far the question I get asked the most.
It's no surprise—with more than a trillion dollars in
student debt currently outstanding in the United States, it
ranks just below home mortgages as the largest source
of personal debt in the country. The cost of college has

but the job prospects for graduates

ace.

are only open to you after several

n. If being a doctor or a lawyer is

need to go to college. College

..ake connections in your chosen field.

a lot of fun. A college degree gives you

.ptions if you're looking to make a decent income

..uring your work career. Many jobs require a degree of some kind, even those jobs that have nothing to do with anything you might learn in college. Not having one can definitely put you at a disadvantage in future job hunts.

So is it worth piling on debt for a piece of paper?

If you plan on being a working stiff until you're almost seventy, absolutely. The tens or hundreds of thousands of dollars in debt will, eventually, be surpassed by your earnings, and somewhere in the next forty years you'll come out ahead.

If you want to be rich by thirty, the math is different.

Don't believe the fiction that you're doomed to a life of manual labor and poverty if you skip college. Knowing how to make money is worth more than any degree, and those pieces of paper mean very little when you start working for yourself.

WHY YOU SHOULDN'T WORK FOR OTHER PEOPLE

As long as you work for other people, your income will be determined by someone who is incentivized to get the most work out of you for as little pay as possible. This dynamic is true in every field. Having a boss means

101

having your annual salary decided by someone other than yourself.

Job security is an oxymoron. As long as you're working for someone else, many factors of your continued employment are out of your control. If company profits start to slip because of decisions at the top, people at the middle and bottom are the first ones to go. Even large, established companies go through rounds of restructuring and layoffs.

Advancement will always be difficult. There's a catch-22 about working your way up the corporate ladder. Nobody wants to put you in charge of something until you have experience, but you can't get experience if nobody will put you in charge.

There's only one way around all of this, and that's starting your own business. Even if it's not your primary source of income, the experience you get from starting a business makes you more valuable as an employee. Your business may only provide some extra spending cash, or it might grow to be your primary source of income. The limit is your creativity and ability, not an arbitrary number dictated by your employer.

It's also another layer of security. If you end up losing your job, you've got something to fall back on. Even a small business is an income stream to tide you over until you find a better job with your new list of qualifications.

GETTING THERE

Maybe you're not in a position to start your own business yet. Businesses have start-up costs, and while most of the business models I suggest don't require much capital up front, you'll still need some cash. Even if you never start your own business you should at least learn how to make more money as an employee.

The first thing you need to do is go over your resume, because it's probably a bunch of garbage at the moment.

It's not your fault. You just wrote it the way you've been told to write a resume, which is completely wrong.

In school they tell you *how* to write resumes, but not *why*. I remember being taught the importance of formatting, and that I should always put a "statement of intent" at the top of a resume. I should list every job and a description of what I did, as well as any extracurricular activities and awards I've received. It should be no more than two pages and include references. A hiring manager should be able to read through your resume and have a good understanding of your full work history.

If that's how you write your resume, you will not get hired.

While I try to automate everything with my own businesses so I don't have to pay anyone, I have been in the role of hiring manager many times. I can tell you this: nobody cares about your babysitting job. Your extracurricular activities are irrelevant, unless you just so happen to share an interest with me. Then we can talk about it at the interview. But I'm still not going to hire you.

I don't care what you did two or three jobs ago if it doesn't tell me how well you'll do at the job I'm hiring for.

I will hire a dull, boring high school dropout with no hobbies or relevant experience if I'm convinced doing so will make me money. I will pass over an Ivy League graduate with a 4.0 GPA if I don't think they have the drive or creativity required to help my company grow.

Your resume is an advertisement, not a historical document. It's not a way to tell a potential employer all the things you've done. It's a way to show them very specific things in your past that will help you succeed at the job they're hiring for.

You don't have to list your job responsibilities in the order of the time you spent doing them. If you spent just 10 percent of your time at your last job doing something relevant to the position you want, list that first.

When a hiring manager pulls up your resume, you've got about ten seconds to convince her of your qualifications before she moves on to the next applicant. Don't waste any of that time with irrelevant information.

Make a few different versions of your resume, each targeting a different type of job you want. It'll save you a lot of time when you start sending them out in bulk.

JOB HOP

So you've landed a job. Fantastic. Now start looking for another one.

The idea of starting at the bottom and working your way up is quaint and outdated. Like people, companies believe the grass is greener on the other side and often hire outside of the company to fill positions. If you're good at your job, they have very little incentive to promote you.

Always remember that, even as an employee, you are your own boss. You are working for yourself. Regardless of who signs your paycheck, you are the one responsible for getting out of bed every day to go to work and build your future. Learn all you can at your job, advance as far as you can at your job, and then leave.

The best time to look for a job is when you already have one.

If you can make more money somewhere else, do it. Always be looking for opportunities. Your job isn't your girlfriend. It's not your husband. It's a temporary agreement that can be terminated by either side, and no matter what, it will be terminated at some point. Make sure it's on your terms.

Some people have a problem with this mentality. I've talked to a number of people who know they should find another job but stay out of a sense of loyalty. I don't know you, and I don't know your employer, but I can tell you with 99 percent certainty that if the person running the company you work for decided he could make more money without you, you'd be out of a job tomorrow.

"Chaos is a ladder."
—Petyr Baelish, *Game of Thrones*

People who want security like to work for large companies. If you're starting at the bottom and want to work your way up quickly, there's no worse place to work. I could not have gone from administrative assistant to director of marketing in a year by working at a large, established corporation.

One of the fastest ways to improve your resume and take giant leaps up the corporate ladder is to work for small companies and start-ups. There's risk involved, especially with start-ups, as they have unproven business models and could run out of money at any time. It also means they don't have an entrenched leadership structure, so there's plenty of opportunity to move up.

If you go to your boss at a small start-up and ask why your company doesn't have anyone in charge of social media, there's a good chance you'll walk away as your company's new social media manager. Go home and put it on your resume.

Prove your worth, ask for more responsibility, and keep checking job listings. Keep job hopping, gaining experience, and improving your income until you can be in the best position of all—the one where nobody above you is worried how much money you make.

Of course, you need to apply some common sense. If you've had three different jobs in the past six months, it's not going to look good on your resume.

As a rule of thumb, don't stay in one place for more than two years unless you're actively moving up or learning skills that will pay off on your next job switch.

I decided to always be in over my head when finding a new job. As soon as I got to the point where I could tread water, it was time to move on to the next challenge.

"HOW MUCH ARE YOU CURRENTLY MAKING?"

This question invariably comes up in every job interview. An employer wants to know this for obvious reasons. First, it gives him an idea of your market value. If he decides to hire you, he wants to offer you just enough above what you're currently making to get you to switch.

When negotiating salary, you don't want to be the first person to throw out a number. It's especially true if the job listing didn't mention a salary range. The company might expect to pay $60,000 for the job, but if you speak first and say you're looking for $40,000, they're going to offer you $40,000.

Turn the question around. Ask the interviewer what they were looking to pay someone for the position.

If you must answer first, be honest but creative. If you charge a solid hourly rate as a freelancer, mention that you're looking for compensation that matches your higher-paid side job. If you're doing it right, the job you're interviewing for will be a substantial step up in salary, and you'll need to convince the hiring manager that you're worth it.

NETWORK

My financial life has been impacted more by short conversations over lunch than all the planning and hard work I've done put together.

Honestly, this may be more of a "which came first, the chicken or the egg?" situation, because without the planning and hard work those conversations wouldn't have happened. Without those conversations, though, all that hard work wouldn't have paid off.

When your boss asks if you want to go to lunch, always say yes. Go to conferences, trade shows, and meetups relevant to your industry. Don't miss any opportunity to network.

When you quit a job, always, always, *always* leave with grace. It doesn't matter if you're a lawyer at a top firm or a line cook at McDonald's. It doesn't matter how wronged you feel or how justified you think you are in cussing out half the company. You never know when you'll come across the same people again in your career, and not burning bridges costs you nothing. It doesn't matter if you think the company is doing everything wrong—you're on your way out and don't have to worry about it anymore.

Like most people, there have been times when I've wanted to leave a job in a blaze of glory. I wanted to let everyone know what I really thought of them. This is a bad idea.

Sit on it. Smile in the exit interview.

I've done this every time, and it's lead to many opportunities years later.

WHEN YOU'RE READY TO LEAVE, ASK FOR A RAISE

If you're at your breaking point with your current job and have decided to leave, stop and think about how much money it would take to get you to stay.

Since you've already decided you don't need the job, what's the harm in asking for the extra money? At worst they say no, and you quit. At best they say yes, you work another six months while looking for another job with your new, higher salary, and then quit.

This is another reason why it's important to be in a job where you're close to the money. If it's easy for your boss to imagine the amount of money the company would lose if you left, you have a lot of room to negotiate. A lot of people want jobs where they're not constantly measured and evaluated, where their take-home pay isn't tied to any financial success metrics. These people will not be rich anytime soon.

You want a position where your employer knows exactly how valuable you are, and when it comes time to ask for a raise, all you need to do is present a spreadsheet.

It doesn't have to be sales. Marketing and business development are solid choices, but even a social media manager can make a lot of money if she can show how increased engagement with the company's social media accounts is leading to more sales.

Regardless of your current position, if you're ever at the point where you'd be comfortable leaving a job, that's exactly the time to ask for more money. It puts you in a strong position to negotiate because, in your mind, you're already out the door.

ASK FOR TOO MUCH

One of the benefits of working for myself was that it allowed me to try out new hobbies, one of which was high-stakes poker. From Las Vegas, Nevada, to Macau, China, I've sat at poker tables and watched as hundreds of thousands of dollars changed hands in an instant. I've usually folded by the time that happens, but I've learned a lot by playing the game at such high stakes.

In poker, position is power. The last person to act has the best position and the most power. They get to sit back and watch what everyone else does before they're forced to make a move. Weak hands very often beat strong hands if the player with the weaker hand has the stronger position.

Not having to act is one of the most powerful positions you can be in. If you're looking for a new job while you still have one, you can ask your potential new employer for anything you like. You already have a job. If they say no, you're no worse off than you were the week before.

Always negotiate from strength. That means not waiting until you're unemployed to look for a better job. You want to go into the job interview on your terms.

I've often used the position of not having to act to make more money. After my side projects had grown enough for me to start working for myself full-time, I received a number of job offers. I didn't want to take any of them.

Instead of saying no, I came up with a ridiculous number in my head that would be enough for me to go back to work for someone else. Many times I was actually embarrassed to ask for the amount in my head, because it didn't match the work I was being asked to do. Since I didn't want to do the work, though, there was no harm in asking for too much. If they said no, I wouldn't have to come up with an excuse to turn them down. If they said yes, I'd be stuck working for a boss again, but I'd have a big pile of money to console me until I couldn't stand it anymore.

I was surprised by how often they said yes.

WHO ARE YOU WORKING FOR?

Never forget that, even when you have a job, you're not working for your employer. You are working for yourself.

You're a contractor with a product (your time) that you sell, but your ultimate responsibility is to yourself.

It's up to you to look out for your career advancement, not your boss. Passively waiting to be recognized and rewarded is a losing strategy.

Your primary job is to always be a salesman for yourself.

START A BUSINESS, ANY BUSINESS

Want to be a journalist? Start your own publication. Do you hang drywall for a living? Find a good plumber and electrician, then start a general contracting company.

There's no better way to advance your career than by starting your own business. Even if you keep your day job, you'll learn how your boss thinks and gain invaluable skills you'd never learn as an employee.

There are many other benefits to creating your own company. Depending on the industry, you can end up with a ton of tax write-offs. Running your own side business is also a great way to cover any gaps in your work history. If you find yourself in between jobs, work on your business while sending out resumes. Then you don't have to say you were unemployed; instead, you can say you were working for yourself. That sounds much better to a potential employer.

Ideally, your side business will eventually become your main job. If you build it the right way, you'll be able to outsource and automate until there's little to do but enjoy your income.

There are other perks to having your own business. Of course, there's the business cards you'll get printed off with your name and "CEO" at the top, but the end goal of having your own business is living a lifestyle of your choosing.

Traveling is very important to me, so when I started my own company, my goal was to automate any task that didn't involve going somewhere interesting. Whether it's a conference in Amsterdam, a corporate party in New York, or a seminar in London, I'm able to take regular business trips without having too much work pile up. The business part of the trip takes up a few hours of each day, and I get the rest of the time to explore. I wanted to see the world, so I built the business to give me a lifestyle based on travel.

Maybe you're more of a homebody and would love nothing more than to work from your couch. If you have a boss, the option to telecommute is always up to someone else, but if it's your company, you can build it from the ground up so that you never have to go to an office.

Even if you never reach the point where you can sustain yourself with income from your own company, starting a business is still one of the best decisions you can make. I think everyone should be an entrepreneur, but that doesn't mean everyone should do it full-time.

It's an education in making money that you won't get anywhere else, and it has the potential to boost your earnings far higher than any degree.

EXPERIENCE

Following this path and job hopping between start-ups gives you more than just work experience. You'll also experience different workplace cultures that will challenge the way you view the world, business, and money in general.

I used all of these techniques to grow my annual income from $14,000 to over $1 million.

At twenty-four I was working for a government contracting company as an administrative assistant making $8 an hour. I'd worked at that job part-time for several years because it was easy and low stress, with a fairly flexible work schedule. It was also very boring, but I was comfortable and I didn't think I could do better without a degree.

Then I decided to run my experiment and see if I could double my income every year.

The first step was easy. I was making so little that doubling it wasn't too hard. I spent a few months sending out resumes, and because I already had a job, I could apply for positions I had very little chance of getting but that paid substantially more. I eventually landed a job as an executive assistant at a biometrics start-up that paid twice as much as I'd been making.

The change in culture was shocking. There were new hires every other week. Project timelines were a couple of weeks, not six months to a year. There was a soda fountain in the kitchen.

A few months after I started the job, the company was bought out by their only competitor. The new bosses were on the other side of the country, and our former CEO disappeared to the Caribbean with his new fortune. Someone brought a keg of beer to a company picnic one weekend. The same keg showed up at the office the following Monday. The red Solo cups from the kitchen were no longer filled with soda.

I'd been afraid to venture out into the unknown, but here I was making twice as much in a job that was even less stressful than the one I'd left. Still, it was obvious the party wasn't going to last forever, so I started to form an exit plan.

I updated my resume. Though I'd been hired as an executive assistant, I was put in charge of the reseller program in addition to my normal work. Most of what I put on my resume was related to the marketing initiatives I developed to assist our affiliates as the reseller director. I did not talk about the time I had to print off pictures of the CEO and his girlfriend, make them into little flags, and put them on top of cupcakes for their anniversary. I left out the part where it was my job to bring coffee and doughnuts to all company meetings. In fact, I left out most of the duties required of an executive assistant.

I didn't include those things because I did not want to do those things at my next job.

After sending out a few hundred resumes, I took a minor pay cut to work at another start-up as a director of marketing. Though the job paid less, I took it to add the title to my resume.

The owner liked the work I'd done while in charge of the reseller program at my previous position. On my resume, I also included all the work I'd done to promote my own book. I played up the fact that it was all done on a shoestring budget through social media and guerilla marketing. That impressed him, primarily because he didn't want to spend a lot of money promoting his product. There was no talk of fetching coffee.

That job was how I ended up in Vegas, at a launch party broken up by cavalry, surrounded by white tigers and go-go dancers. The party was thrown by a local distributor of our energy drink product. The distributor flew me and all of my coworkers out to Las Vegas, put us up in suites at The Venetian, got us pit tickets to a NASCAR race, invited us to a launch party at a rented mansion, and when the party got raided, they took us out to clubs and bought bottles of champagne and liquor all night. The entire weekend was parties and limos.

A few weeks after we got back from Las Vegas, the distributor bought our company and laid us all off.

By now I realized this came with the territory. I was unemployed, but my prospects had improved tremendously.

I spent the next couple of months sending off dozens of resumes every day, highlighting my experience as a director of marketing. I got a bite from a company in DC that was looking for a search engine optimization manager. The job listing showed it paid more than double my previous job. I tweaked my resume to highlight how I'd gotten my self-published book to show at the top of Google searches when people typed in keywords like "self-published author."

I'd never taken a class in search engine optimization. At the time, classes for it didn't exist. While I'd learned a lot about SEO on my own, I had no relevant job experience.

I also had never spoken to anyone with an SEO background. I knew the concepts but not the language—I couldn't talk the talk.

The day before the interview, I bought and read an *SEO For Dummies* book.

Okay, I only skimmed it. I looked for keywords and important acronyms I should know. When I walked into the interview the next day, the For Dummies book was my only formal SEO training.

THE INTERVIEW

Brad was silent.

He stared at the resume for a moment before turning it over. There was nothing on the back.

"Am I missing a page?"

I knew he was confused because I hadn't listed any educational history. The job listing said a degree in marketing was preferred, and I had barely passed high school.

"No, I didn't go to college. I decided to start working after high school."

He was silent again.

Education wasn't the only qualification I didn't have. None of my previous jobs involved search engine optimization, which is something companies usually look for when hiring someone to manage their SEO program.

Not only did my work history leave me completely unqualified for the job, but I'd also been unemployed for months. Noticing the employment gap, Brad asked me what I'd been up to.

Up until this point, things had not been going well. Here's how I got the job:

"I've been promoting my book," I said truthfully.

I then told him how I'd written a fiction novel.

I published it myself.

I marketed it myself.

I had thirty-two thousand people following me on social media. Social media was still relatively new (this was the Myspace era) and thirty-two thousand was a big number at the time.

I e-mailed those fans and asked them to distribute tens of thousands of bookmarks I'd printed up with the name of the book. They left them at coffee shops and libraries across the country.

This guerilla marketing help my book land, however briefly, on the top 100 best sellers list on Amazon.

I brought a different book to the interview. It was a marketing book by an author I'd never met, but several pages of the book were about me. The author had included a case study of my success in using new online marketing channels to promote my book.

Still, I might not have gotten the job if it had ended there.

Brad's laptop was on the table, so I told him to Google "self-published author." The first result was an article about me. Since the job would be to make sure his company's website appeared at the top of search results on Google, that sealed the deal.

It was my work as an entrepreneur, working for myself and being my own boss, that got me a better job, not a degree and a well-formatted resume.

There was just one more hurdle.

"How much did you make at your last job?" Brad asked.

Again, I told the truth. I mentioned the $30,000 salary at my last job but that, because it was a start-up, I'd been offered additional compensation based on the growth of the company.

Still, to make the point clear I added:

"This is closer to what I'm doing for myself currently than what I was doing at my last job. Based on that, I'd be looking for something around $72,000."

I said "72" to make it seem like I'd put a lot of thought into the number. In reality, I was just waiting to get laughed out of the room.

Brad was silent again. I knew I'd pushed it too far. I was in over my head.

"Shouldn't be a problem," Brad said.

Weeks later, their HR department finally gave me a call and offered me $60,000 a year—double my previous salary.

I was ecstatic.

I told them no. I was sorry, but I couldn't do it for less than $72,000. "Brad mentioned it wouldn't be a problem," I added.

The next day I had an offer letter for the full $72,000.

My new perspective on money had been vindicated.

Who is a company more likely to hire, a person with a PhD in search engine optimization (I'm pretty sure that doesn't exist), or someone who can show they've been able to get websites to the top of Google's search results?

Nothing matters aside from showing you can do the job and either make the company more money or make the person hiring you look good so he can make more money.

This was my shot, and I took as much responsibility as they'd give me.

After driving home, I'd work until two a.m. most days. While I'd been hired to manage the company's search engine optimization, within a few months I was managing a paid-search marketing budget of $3 million a month.

That made it easy to show my worth to the company. I was able to cut the marketing budget in half while increasing revenue. After a year on the job, I walked into Brad's office and asked him to triple my salary.

I had the numbers to back it up. I was not the smartest person at the company, and I wasn't the hardest working, but I could point to the millions of dollars a month the company was making from my efforts because my job was close to the money. It wasn't an emotional appeal, it was simply me showing that paying me more and keeping me with the company benefited both him and the business in the long run. My argument did not involve smooth talking (which I'm not good at anyway); it instead relied on decisions I'd started making twelve months before walking into my boss's office.

I walked out with my salary doubled and bonuses tied to future performance. I hit every goal over the next year and, with the bonuses, ended up securing the 200 percent raise I'd asked for.

A BULL IN A CHINA CLOSET

To be successful, you're going to have to step outside of your comfort zone. By nature I'm introverted and mild mannered. I'm a listener and observer. These traits can be beneficial, but there are times when you need to be more forward and direct.

When I was an executive assistant, I asked my boss if I could sit in on marketing meetings. I took notes and went to my boss with suggestions. When I presented a good idea, I was usually given more marketing work to do (which helped build my resume). When I presented a bad idea, I was told why it wouldn't work. It was humbling, but it was also a free education.

At a later job, I overheard the CEO in my boss's office talking about a new marketing initiative. I heard bits and pieces, and it caught my interest, so I opened the door and walked into the office. Both of them stared at me as I sat down in an empty seat.

"I figured since I was going to be eavesdropping I might as well do it in here," I said.

I realized right away how arrogant I sounded and cringed a bit inwardly.

The CEO stared at me for another moment. Then he laughed. "I like that," he said and then included me in the discussion.

The same CEO would later call me a bull in a china closet. He would also give final approval for my $150,000 raise.

Before you get the wrong idea, these actions don't match my personality type at all. It was terrifying. If I'd gone with my instincts, I would have sat at my desk for years trying to look as small as possible (especially after the chair throwing incident) and collect a paycheck.

PASSIVE INCOME

It's possible to make a very comfortable living as an employee. It's also possible to find a job with enough flexibility to provide the work-life balance you desire. No matter how good the job is, though, you'll always be dependent on someone else to set your salary, hours, and responsibilities. Since you're at the mercy of others, your livelihood is always at risk.

The Holy Grail of personal finance is creating enough passive income to live comfortably without working for other people. It's the only way to truly become self-reliant and finally eliminate the risks that come from being an employee.

Passive income is generated from large investments in companies or real estate. It can also come from owning a business that's structured to create passive income. So if you don't have a giant pile of cash sitting around your house, there's really only one option—you need to start a business. Remember that while the wealthy can invest money, the poor must invest time. If you don't already have a large bank account, investing the time to build a business is the way to go.

The less cash you have to start your business, the more footwork you'll have to do yourself. This can be to your benefit, as you'll learn more about your business by building it from the ground up.

In the next few chapters, we'll work on making the transition from employee to business owner. I'll also go over automating and outsourcing your responsibilities until you have complete control of your time. If you're looking to build a life you don't need to take a vacation from, these are the steps you need to take to make it happen.

CHAPTER 6

OUTSOURCING, AUTOMATION, AND PASSIVE INCOME

There are many reasons for wanting to be rich, but I'm going to assume these two are near the top of your list:

You don't want to worry about money.
You want more control over when you work
(setting your own hours, having more time for family and friends, etc.).

A lot of the information in this book can be used to help you increase your salary as an employee, but if you want to be truly rich (and have the lifestyle many of us think about when we hear the word "wealthy"), you're going to have to start your own business.

The vast majority of the super wealthy own or started a business. In the United States, two-thirds of non-retired millionaires are self-employed. A person who is self-employed is four times more likely to be a millionaire. This shouldn't come as a surprise—as long as you're an employee, there will always be someone above you trying to figure out how to get more work out of you for less money.

About a year after I got that huge raise, the investment firm that owned the company started looking for ways to cut the budget. When they went through the numbers, they saw a twentysomething kid pulling in almost a quarter million dollars a year and figured that was a good place to start.

Showing value is the best way to get ahead in business, but there's no guarantee some number cruncher isn't going to come along with an idea to save the company a few bucks—*your* bucks.

So they cut my pay. In the end, it turned out to be the best thing they could have done. The pay cut (as well as one particularly ugly incident with my boss) convinced me I had to work for myself.

As long as someone was worried about how much I was making, I'd never make as much as I wanted.

Sure, it's possible you'll end up as the CEO of a multinational corporation with hundreds of millions of dollars in stock options and a golden parachute—but don't hold your breath. Remember, you only get one lifetime, and that's not a good gamble to take.

Let's look at more realistic situations.

A lawyer who works for a firm can only earn so much money. A lawyer with his own firm who hires other lawyers to work for him doesn't have the same limits.

A carpenter can only earn so much money. A general contractor who hires carpenters and other workers doesn't have the same limits.

As an employee, you're paid for the work you do. As a business owner, you can get paid for the work other people do. There's only so much work an individual can do in a day, so if you're getting paid for your labor, there is a hard cap on how much you can make. If you've got people (or computers) working for you, you remove that limitation.

Of course, hiring people isn't cheap. In addition to their salary, there's the cost of recruiting, training, health insurance premiums, and unemployment insurance. The more workers you have, the more liability you have. Managing workers can also create more work for their employer.

That's why I usually look for opportunities with high-revenue and high-automation potential.

AUTOMATION (Or, *OMG, We're All Going To Be Replaced By Robots!*)

There are two main reasons the rich have gotten richer in the past few decades.

The first is global trade. A company's market is no longer limited by geography. Instead of selling to people in the immediate area, a single online storefront has more than seven billion potential customers.

A company that's gone from millions in revenue to billions on the strength of global trade still only has one CEO and, for private companies, a limited number of owners. There's a bigger pie for those at the top to split.

The second reason the rich are getting richer is automation. The costs to do business have not scaled at the same rate as the growth in customers. Thanks to technology, companies can serve the global economy without hiring more people.

While some people see this as a wonderful opportunity, it has a lot of other people downright terrified.

There's been a lot of talk lately about the effect technological advances and automation in general will have on the workforce. Many people are worried that they will eventually be replaced by a machine.

They're right.

Whatever your job is today, there's a good chance technology will replace it or make it obsolete.

We know this because technology has already put everyone out of work. In fact, it's done so repeatedly.

A hundred years ago, the number-one occupation in America was farming. Then technology and automation came along and took everyone's job. Today, only about 2 percent of Americans work in farming.

The terrible consequence of these mass layoffs? We now have more food than ever. There's more variety, and we have more money to spend on buying it.

But... but this is different, say the technophobes. It's not.

Automation put bowling pin setters out of a job.

Refrigeration put milkmen out of a job.

Switchboard operators are a thing of the past.

Door-to-door salesmen are gone.

"Typist" is another formerly common profession that doesn't exist anymore.

File clerks have mostly disappeared. Several of my jobs when I was younger involved sitting in a room and filing paperwork and folders away on giant shelves. Now those folders only exist on a computer.

Elevator operators are out of work.

The postal service has shrunk considerably since the advent of e-mail.

It's likely that the people taking your order at fast-food restaurants are next on the chopping block. In many places, they're already being replaced by self-serve kiosks.

With all these jobs disappearing, you'd think the United States would have massive unemployment.

The unemployment rate a hundred years ago was 5.6 percent. At the end of last year, it was 5 percent.

In place of all these lost jobs are careers nobody could have imagined a century ago.

A migrant worker in the early twentieth century had no idea his grandchild would be a social network marketer. He couldn't have imagined *app developer* or *YouTube content creator* would ever become professions. I have no idea what jobs are going to exist when my grandchildren enter the workplace, but it will probably be higher paying and cushier than most of the jobs available today.

Now, all that just means is that, as a whole, we'll be fine. However, that's of very little comfort if your job has just been automated and you're no longer needed. This is why the best thing you can do is to be your own boss.

Automation isn't going to stop. If you are your own boss, you're not going to lay yourself off. If you do find a way to automate your own job, you can just sit back and let the profits roll in.

We all have a choice. We can complain about automation and technology, or we can use it to make more wealth than has ever existed until now.

The people who will be poor in the future are today worried that automation will put them out of a job. The people who will be rich in the future are today figuring out how they can use automation to start and run a business with less overhead than ever before.

I started my first company with $6,000 on a credit card. Aside from occasional contractors, I never hired any

127

employees while the company grew to more than $4 million a year in revenue. My biggest overhead cost was IT. It cost me $600 a month to run a website with more than a million monthly visitors.

Those numbers never would have been possible in a world where I had to pay rent for a physical store and hire enough staff to deal with a million customers.

OUTSOURCING

Outsourcing isn't just about sending jobs overseas. It's a way to take things off your plate that can't be 100 percent automated by technology, regardless of where the work is actually done. I've yet to hire a full-time employee for any of my companies, but that doesn't mean I'm not creating jobs here at home.

The companies I work with have hired more employees to handle the additional business I've sent them. Some of these companies I've contracted to do work for me; others I have an affiliate relationship with, and I sell their products.

Most of the jobs I've created indirectly are in the United States, with some in the UK and India. I've got the best of both worlds. I have people working for me all over the globe, but I don't have to manage a single employee.

The expenses, the drama, the headaches—all of these have been outsourced to other people. I built my business from the ground up to have as few people as possible involved directly.

I never have to fire anyone. I don't need to put anyone on a performance improvement plan. I don't need to yell at anyone for showing up to work late.

Unlike most medium and large businesses, I don't have to pay for health insurance. I don't need to pay Social Security for my employees. I don't need to pay the unemployment insurance tax.

I have far fewer liabilities. I don't need to worry about getting sued for sexual harassment by a disgruntled employee (which is great because I seldom wear pants to the "office"). I can have a completely unsafe work environment, and nobody cares!

Outsourcing is essential to escaping the grind and living on your own terms.

AUTOMATION AND SCALE

Many people leave their jobs to strike out on their own only to become an employee all over again.

My dad was an entrepreneur. He opened a restaurant and worked his hardest to make it successful. He was a cook, a bookkeeper, a dishwasher, and a marketer. He worked harder than he would have at any day job, and he kept it up for a decade.

I have a deep respect for my father and his work ethic, but later in life I realized (and he did, too) that taking on that level of work can actually prevent you from building a business empire.

He had no room to scale. There are only so many hours in a day, and he was using all of them.

The biggest irony in business is that, to be successful, you have to find ways to work less.

If you've been to a major city, there's a good chance you've eaten at a restaurant with a celebrity chef's name on it. I guarantee you that celebrity chef was not the one who cooked your food.

If you're the person making the food, you're just another employee, even if your name is on the building. If you're a cog in your own machine, you can't leave to work on something else without the machine breaking down.

That's why a celebrity chef will open a restaurant, design a menu, then hire someone to cook the food while they go to another city and start the process all over again.

You need to do the same thing. Design a product and let someone else make it. Create a business model and let other people handle the day-to-day operations.

If you're a professional blogger writing your own articles, you're acting like a journalist, not a business owner. You'll never make more than an employee. Find a way to source content scalably and you go from journalist to media mogul.

NO INVENTORY = LOW START-UP COSTS

I'd argue that the best thing technology has done for business owners is to allow them to sell things that don't exist. In more than a decade of working for myself and selling products to the public I've never held a single piece of inventory.

There are many ways to start an inventory-free business. Some people earn millions of dollars a year making YouTube videos. Others sell products like e-books that can be reproduced to infinity at virtually no cost and don't accrue storage fees in a warehouse.

There's one place where automation, scalability, outsourcing and inventory-avoidance combine to create the perfect conditions for a lifestyle business. It's a model built for people who want to own a business without building everything from scratch. No product design, no shopping for manufacturers, no quality testing, no shipping, no storage, no customer service, nothing. It's just a business in a box with very low start-up costs; a turnkey solution called *affiliate marketing*.

AFFILIATE MARKETING

Affiliate marketing is, essentially, selling other people's stuff. Someone else has done the heavy lifting to create a product and the support structure behind it. You get paid a percentage to sell their product.

There are drawbacks to the business model— mainly that you're splitting profits with another company—but on the upside, the other company handles nearly all of the day-to-day tasks associated with running a business, as well as the costs involved.

I couldn't start the next Walmart or Amazon. I don't have the time or money I'd need to invest to create such a retail behemoth. Luckily for me (and you), I don't have to when I can sell their stuff and get paid for it.

It's not just big-box retailers, either. For just about any product you're interested in selling, there's a company out there already running an affiliate program for it.

If you have your heart set on building your own brand and not promoting a giant corporation, you can do that, too. White-label affiliate programs allow you to sell another company's product with your name on it. It could be a physical product like a bottle of shampoo with your label on the side, or it could be a service that you sell through your own website under your own brand, but everything from credit card processing to fulfillment and customer service is handled by someone else.

To make affiliate marketing work, it's important to find the right deal. The Amazon affiliate program is great because you can sell just about anything, but the payouts are extremely low. Amazon has very low profit margins, and that translates into low payouts for affiliates.

If you're selling a specific product, it's better to go to a manufacturer and work out a deal. This cuts out a middleman and leaves more profit to be split.

When looking around for affiliate programs to join, keep in mind that the published payout rates are not a final number. To get a good idea of what's available, check out a few affiliate networks like Commission Junction or Impact Radius. Affiliate networks are a great place to find leads, but many of these networks take as much as a third of a company's affiliate payouts for themselves. That means there's a lot of room to negotiate if you're able to strike a direct deal with the company and bypass the affiliate network.

Your best friend when negotiating a direct affiliate deal is sales volume. It's important you don't sign a contract up front for a specific amount of time (greater than, say, a month). At the start of your business relationship, the company you are now an affiliate of has no idea how much of their product you'll be able to sell, so their payouts likely reflect the belief that you'll be like most affiliates and sell very little.

Set everything up ahead of time so you can hit the ground running. Sell as much as you can as fast as you can, even if it's not sustainable. (If you're doing this with paid advertising, don't risk more than you're willing to lose. It's very easy to lose a lot of money quickly by being too aggressive.) When you've hit your sales peak, shut it all down. All of it. No more sales.

Strange, I know, but this is an effective tactic. It won't work with a company the size of Amazon, but for most other businesses, it's a great way to get a better deal. High sales volume, even over a short period of time, shows you're serious about the project. It shows you're not just another one of the hundreds of affiliates who have signed up for the program and never made a single sale. It lets the company know that you're worth working with.

It works because companies get addicted to additional revenue very quickly, and they're willing to negotiate with you to get it back. Secondly, it costs a company less to work with one affiliate that does a lot of business than many small affiliates. To get the sales, they'll likely be willing to share that savings with you.

When I started my first business as an affiliate marketer, I joined an affiliate program with a very low payout structure, but I was sure there was a lot of room to negotiate. I pushed as hard as I could the first month and lost money on purpose. I bought traffic from Google and paid twice as much per customer as I was getting paid.

After a week, I was the company's largest affiliate partner. I let the marketing run the whole month, then shut everything down. The next morning, I got a phone call from a freaked-out affiliate manager wanting to know why all their business had dried up.

I was honest. It was costing me double what they were paying me to generate a customer. If they wanted the volume, they'd have to pay me more than double.

I wasn't being greedy, I was being straightforward. I couldn't keep operating at a loss, so they could either pay me a lot more or lose the sales.

Again, I didn't smooth talk my way into a better deal. I was in a solid position because there was no way I was going to budge. Losing money wasn't something I would ever agree to do long term.

They called several times with offers, but in the end gave me what I originally asked for. I turned all the marketing back on that afternoon and have been running it profitably ever since.

I've used this tactic on several occasions, but it can be very risky. Don't do it long term, never spend more than you can afford to lose, and only use it when you have a clear objective in mind. If it's costing you more to acquire a customer than you could ever hope to negotiate per sale, then stop immediately.

LOW-EFFORT INCOME

A lot of people are terrified by the amount of work that goes into building a business. The reality is that, if you're doing it right, it can be easier than a full-time job.

An automated business is the best way for someone who's not already rich to create passive income.

A common mistake a lot of entrepreneurs make is trying to build a brand instead of trying to make money.

There's a huge difference between a business built on branding and one built around direct-response marketing.

If your marketing strategy uses the phrase "word of mouth," tear it up, then burn the pieces.

Brand advertisers can afford to lose money to gain recognition for their brand. You can't. If you spent $2,000 on advertising and didn't make $2,001, you need to find a different advertising channel.

Direct-response marketing is designed to introduce a customer to your product and get them to buy it immediately (or in a short period of time). For businesses without a branding budget, it's the only option available.

With offline marketing (newspapers, billboards, etc.), it's very difficult to track a sale back to the specific marketing spend that generated the transaction. If you're running more than one offline campaign, it's almost impossible to tell how well each one is performing.

Online marketing is the exact opposite. With technology like Google Analytics (which is free), you're able to see how every customer found your website. You can watch the performance of every single ad in real time and adjust your spending toward the advertising that works.

Once you know which channels are profitable for you, it's possible to create "evergreen" campaigns that run indefinitely. Evergreen ads are generic enough (for instance, no holiday messaging like "Labor Day Sale") that they can run all year. Aside from checking their performance every so often, these campaigns can continue to run without a lot of effort on your part.

That leaves you with more time to plan your next business, spend with your family, travel, or do whatever else *you* want to do.

CHAPTER 7

THE EASIEST BUSINESS TO START

Brad never screamed at me. I sat in a cubicle outside his office (and later in my own office, just down the hall) for years and heard an almost daily stream of shouting and expletives pour out through his doorway. Everyone got it sooner or later. Catch him at the wrong time, and you'd get your head bitten off. That I'd managed to avoid his wrath for so long was a source of pride for me.

I bring in a lot of money for the company. That must be why I'm safe.

Turned out it was just dumb luck that I survived as long as I did.

Twenty minutes ago I had asked the wrong question, and now I was getting my head ripped off.

I was sitting in a conference room with a dozen people, every one of them a vice president of the company—except for me. Brad had asked me for a sales projection for the coming year. I wasn't sure if he meant a specific division or the company as a whole, so I asked him to clarify. Somehow this hit a nerve, and he let me have it.

I was shocked at his stamina. Every time I thought he was finished, he'd take a deep breath and start all over again. Twenty minutes in, and he showed no signs of slowing. Veins tensed in his neck and forehead as he continued to scream insults at me.

I couldn't believe it.

I knew everyone else in the office had gotten similar treatment at one point or another, but I figured if I worked hard and put up good numbers I'd never be on the receiving end of a Brad Beratement.

I looked around the room trying to find help, but everyone's eyes were down, pretending not to notice the meeting had turned into an execution. They'd all been here before. They didn't want to say anything and risk becoming the new target.

I couldn't blame them. There was nothing I could do but wait it out.

NO GUARANTEES

Perhaps you've been in a similar situation. Maybe it was in a boardroom; maybe it was in a kitchen or back office. If you work for other people, chances are you'll have unpleasant interactions with your boss from time to time. Hopefully not too often, but this is what happens when you work for other people.

Not only do you have someone above you controlling how much you make, but when you're dependent on somebody else for your livelihood (and the livelihood of your family), you end up taking all manner of abuse with a simple "yes sir" or "yes ma'am."

Every time I think about it now, I wish I'd handed Brad my company laptop and walked out of the room.

At the time, my brain kept telling me I couldn't leave. I didn't believe I could make it on my own without a paycheck. I'd been doing some tests with affiliate marketing, but I couldn't come close to replacing my salary if I walked out the door, no matter how tempting it was.

So I did what I believe most people would do when they need to keep their job. I waited silently for him to finish yelling at me, then I told him I was sorry he felt that way and excused myself.

When I got back to my office, I closed the door and sat silently at my desk.

I was hurt and angry, but I needed to collect my thoughts and figure out where to go from there. I'd known for a long time that I didn't want to be an employee for the rest of my life. That afternoon in the conference room was my final reminder.

No matter how scary you think it is to be an entrepreneur, I want to let you in on a secret: being an employee is scarier. You have no control. You can do your job perfectly, but if the people at the top screw up, you still get laid off. How much you make isn't up to you; it's up to someone whose job consists of getting the most work out of you for as little compensation as possible. To top it all off, you have to be polite when they have a bad day and decide to take it out on you.

You're never safe. There are no guarantees. I have friends who were still with that company a couple years later when it folded for good and never got a paycheck for their last several weeks of work. There's risk no matter which path you choose, so why not pick the one where you get to call the shots?

Entrepreneurship was the path or me. If the thought of working hard your whole life to make other people rich bothers you, then it's probably the path for you, too.

Brad apologized the next day, but my mind was already made up. I knew what I had to do and, more importantly, I did it.

A few months later, I handed in my resignation.

There was no yelling or arguing. In fact, I smiled and wished my boss well. I sincerely thanked him for the opportunity and everything I had learned working under him.

I had a pleasant exit interview with human resources. They asked if I had any complaints. I told them I did not.

I walked around the office and said my goodbyes to coworkers who couldn't believe I'd quit without going to another job.

"I've got it taken care of," I told them.

The next morning I woke up, put on a pot of coffee, and made my commute to the couch. I was in business for myself, and it was the greatest feeling in the world.

I'd finally figured out how to replace my salary with automated income.

LOW COST OF ENTRY

Our parents had it rough. If my dad wanted to open a business, he had to find a physical location and invest $50,000 or more of his own money and then wait months or years before seeing any kind of return. Today, opening a physical business can cost $100,000 or more.

Franchise fees, staff, paperwork, and inventory can push the cost even higher.

Opening an internet business costs a few bucks. You could have one up and running by tonight. If you've got a solid product and a good head for marketing, you could wake up to profits tomorrow morning.

That's an extreme example, but most of the businesses I've started only required a few weeks of research and setup and were profitable within a month. I can usually tell if something is worth pursuing after a few hours of work—I'll put together a bare-bones landing page with an offer I want to promote and then buy a few hundred targeted clicks from Google and Bing. If there's no interest from any of the visitors to the site, I'll scrap the project and move on to the next one. There are far too many profitable ideas to waste time with the rest.

I'll explain paid-search marketing in more detail later. It's my favorite way to test a product because you get immediate results. If you spend a couple hundred bucks and don't see anything happening, you can make adjustments on the fly. You don't have that control with print or TV buys.

Paid-search ads are all text and are free to create. TV ads can cost tens of thousands of dollars to produce, and you usually have to commit to a minimum spend of many more thousands. With paid search, you can spend 20 cents and then shut down the whole campaign if you change your mind.

Since paid search is pull instead of push marketing (you're not spending money to create demand, you're advertising to people already in the market), it's also a great way to gauge interest in your product.

Lastly, paid search is a perfect candidate for automation, which is one of the two most important components in building a business that will give you the lifestyle you want.

DO I NEED INVESTORS?

I get this question a lot, and my answer is always that same:
> *Not if you can help it.*
> Investors mean bosses.
> We don't like bosses.

Find a model that allows you to fund your start-up yourself. Depending on your financial situation, this could rule out quite a lot of options. However, I'd argue that it's best to start small, even if you have access to lots of capital.

I self-funded my first business with a credit card. Even though it was profitable early on, I took extra steps to make sure I wouldn't have to tie up a lot of money.

Cash flow can be a huge problem for start-ups. If you run an inventory-heavy business, not having enough cash on hand can severely limit growth. Even if you're technically profitable, cash flow can still be an issue. I've had monthly marketing bills in the hundreds of thousands of dollars—no matter how much money I was due on paper, if I couldn't pay those bills, I'd be in trouble.

I didn't want any unnecessary limits to the growth of my company, so I did my best to take cash flow out of the equation. Most of the income for my first business came from invoices to a single company, and I worked out terms with them so I got paid every two weeks for all outstanding balances instead of having to wait up to two months (as is the case with typical "net 30" contracts). It was a simple negotiation—I told them, honestly, that if they didn't give me what I was asking for, I wouldn't be able to expand our mutual business.

Getting paid immediately while at the same time being able to put all my expenses on a credit card that I wouldn't have to pay off for a month solved all my cash-flow problems.

Since I never needed cash, I never had to raise money from investors, which means I've never had to answer to anyone. I can do whatever I want with the business. I can set my compensation however I want, and I can work whatever hours I want. I don't need to justify any of it to a corporate board full of people who know very little about the day-to-day operations of my company.

Of course, the best part about self-funding is that you get to keep 100 percent of the profits.

For some companies, self-funding isn't possible. Unless you're sure you've got the next billion-dollar idea, I'd avoid trying to start one of these. You'll spend most of your time begging for money and end up stuck in the same trap you're trying to escape. As soon as you sell part of your company, you become an employee again. For me, being my own boss is paramount. Don't leave your job just to create a more stressful one for yourself.

Speaking of leaving your job, keep your personal cash flow in mind. Don't march in and quit just because your side business is making $100 a day. Most businesses fail. The last thing you want to do is have to beg for your old job back.

Even now, as much as I wish I had handed in my resignation immediately after getting chewed out by my boss, I know it was the right decision to stay. Have a healthy cushion set aside before striking out on your own. For some people, it's entirely possible to set up an automated side business and keep their day job indefinitely, giving them an extra source of income as well as leverage. (It's a lot easier to negotiate when you're not terrified of being fired).

I tried, but I couldn't keep working for other people once I was able to reliably support myself without a job. I found this verse, Matthew 6:24, to appropriately describe the situation:

"No one can serve two masters. Either you will hate the one and love the other, or you will be devoted to the one and despise the other..."

I love being an entrepreneur. I hate not being my own boss.

SCALABILITY

Along with automation, scalability is one of the two most important pieces of the puzzle when it comes to building a business, and they're very closely related. You're probably familiar with the concept of economies of scale—essentially, more output requires less additional work and money.

If you want a custom T-shirt, it might cost you $20. If you order enough of them, though, each additional shirt could be as cheap as $2. It's because a lot of the work is in the setup, not the actual production of the shirt.

Once that work is done, it's easy to keep cranking out more shirts.

The same concept applies to creating a business. Ideally, as you grow a business, each additional customer should require less additional work than the one before. As order sizes increase, the amount of extra work should decrease.

There are plenty of books you can read that will help you become more efficient and decrease the amount of additional work even further.

This isn't good enough.

Consider this: One person can only do so much work. Say it takes you an hour of work to bring in $50. Not bad. However, under your current model, doubling your income would require doubling your work.

That's not a good business model.

If you can't double your current revenue while only marginally adding to your workload, you need to reevaluate your business model.

However, no matter how efficient you are, there is only a finite amount of work one person can do. Even if each additional dollar in revenue only adds a small amount of time to your daily routine, you will eventually cap out.

The goal is to build a system where increasing the output does not require any more work on your part. This means building a perfectly scalable business.

The business models I prefer require zero hours of additional work as the company grows. In fact, most of the businesses I've started require much less work once they're at scale than they did when they were small. I put in more work when my first company was making $1,000 a month than when it was making $250,000.

The scalability we're looking for is only possible with automation. I'll get into automation more soon, but when deciding on a business model, it's important to ask yourself if you'll be able to keep up if the business grows the way you want it to. Besides cash flow, this *time flow* is one of the biggest issues that keeps businesses from growing.

STARTING A LIFESTYLE BUSINESS

Of course, the best business model is one where you don't have to do anything and still make money.

The concept of passive income is an old one, and this model has been open to investors as long as money has been around. It's simple—you take a bunch of money, put it in a company, and if the company does well, you get to sit back and let the cash roll in.

I've read a lot of books that treat this model of passive income as a starting point—basically a rich person tells you to buy a bunch of property or invest a bunch of money in the stock market and live off the returns.

Why didn't the rest of us think of that?

If you're like I was and don't have a bunch of money to start with, you need to find another option. Before you can invest money, you need money to invest. One option is to work at your job for the next few decades, squirreling away a bit of cash every month until you finally have enough money to invest and live off the returns.

Of course, by then you're well into your sixties. Still, it's an option.

The better option is to start your own business.

Ideally, this business will provide you with the funds to live life on your own terms. It should also afford you the free time to enjoy that money. These are the key ingredients of a lifestyle business.

To achieve this, every decision you make should be about getting the maximum amount of profit for the least amount of work possible. This isn't laziness. This is understanding that everyone has limits and it's important to not let them get in the way of earning potential. Before you add any time-consuming process to your business, think about how you'll eventually be able to remove yourself from it.

This is part of a mind-set change entrepreneurs need to make. The idea that more work equals more money has to be thrown out.

When I was an employee, if I worked really hard, the business did well, my boss loved me, and I got *really* lucky, maybe I'd get a 10 percent raise at the end of the year. That was the biggest success I could possibly hope for.

Most of us think on that kind of scale. Get rid of that thinking.

I had the fortune to work around large numbers as an employee, and I saw people do very little work and make millions. As an entrepreneur, there have been times I've worked myself to exhaustion only to watch my business shrink. Other times I've coasted by while profits have doubled.

Money doesn't care how hard you work.

Imagine you're trying to find water in the desert. That's what being an employee is like. You're constantly searching for small streams and puddles. Finding water is

147

hard work and time-consuming. When people go to work for themselves, many of them still stay in the desert looking for water. They spend every day fighting to find tiny drops here and there. When you're the boss, you can look wherever you want. You can go to the rain forest. You just have to know where to find one.

That's one of the reasons why I bristle a bit when people say "stick to what you know" or "follow your passion."

If you're in a desert, stop looking for water. You're wasting your time. Move to a place where water is more abundant. It's always easier to change yourself or your circumstances than the world around you.

Instead of looking for money in your comfort zone, look for places outside your comfort zone where money is easier to find. Sometimes that means teaching yourself a new skill set; sometimes it means switching to an entirely different industry.

DOWN TO BUSINESS

First things first. There are two sides to any business—acquiring customers and fulfillment. You sell someone a product or service, then you deliver that product or service.

If you replace windows, *acquiring customers* means going door to door and selling your service. *Fulfillment* means replacing the windows.

As a business owner, your job is to:

Do the work to get the customers
Do the work to replace the windows.

148

When I started a business, I wasn't interested in following that dynamic. I didn't want to replace my job with multiple new jobs. I decided I would delegate, automate, or negotiate my way out of as much work as possible.

FULFILMENT

What I'm going to say next might shock you.

Many profitable businesses don't actually do anything.

We live in a world of middlemen. These are people and companies whose sole job is to connect people who want to do business. Then they take a percentage of the transaction. While we like to believe technology has made the economy more efficient over the years, the truth is, there's never been a better time to be a middleman.

Some connect investors to investment opportunities; some connect businesses to other businesses for the purpose of buyouts or other deals.

The middlemen we're going to talk about are the ones that get customers for other companies and get paid for it. Sometimes this is called white labeling, sometimes it's called affiliate marketing. The only difference is which company's logo is shown to the customer.

The company I worked for that sold cell phones online had two lines of business. One was selling to consumers, the other was handling fulfilment for large companies that were also selling to consumers. This second line of business was so big that, for a few years, if you ordered a cell phone from any major company online (besides the wireless carriers themselves), chances are this one company was actually sending you your phone.

For instance, if you went to the wireless section of Walmart.com and bought a phone with a carrier plan, the order flow would look the same as any other order you might place on the site. Instead of going to Walmart, though, the information would come to us. We'd perform the credit check. We'd activate the phone with the carrier. We'd ship it to the customer.

Walmart took a healthy cut of the transaction without ever touching the product.

There was some upfront work to integrate our company's code into Walmart's website, but after that, it didn't matter if Walmart sold one phone or a million. There was no additional work for them no matter how much additional revenue was generated.

This is the way large swaths of our economy work. Deals are cut, money changes hands, and only one party does the work.

So why is this important to you?

You don't have to be Walmart to get these deals. When I went into the travel business, it only took me a few minutes to find white label solutions that allowed me to have my own customer-facing brand while all the work of running a travel agency was done by somebody else. There was no start-up cost, no minimum booking commitments. I built an extremely simple website, plugged in their code, and I was ready to start selling. The other company handled everything from billing to booking to customer service. After my order volume grew, they even rebuilt my very amateurish website to make it look more respectable at no cost.

White label solutions are available in almost any industry. That's the route to go if you want to build your own brand but skip most of the day-to-day work of running a company. If you're not interested in building your own brand, there's an affiliate program that will allow you to sell just about anything you can imagine.

As a starting point, check out programs like Amazon Associates and Commission Junction. They're a great way to learn the game, but down the road you'll want to do direct deals with service or product providers. Just because you're a middleman doesn't mean you have to use them.

There are a few alternatives to affiliate marketing that require more work but have the potential to give you better margins.

Drop-shipping has a lot in common with white labeling. You manage the store but don't actually own the inventory. When you get an order, you basically forward it to the supplying company who in turn sends the product to the customer. You get your cut of the transaction, which is often around half of the purchase price, though this varies wildly depending on the product.

You don't have to use a third party for your fulfillment. If you're able to avoid it, the percentage you get to keep from each sale can go up dramatically. However, there are a few things to keep in mind if you go it alone.

You don't want a product that requires a lot of customer contact, unless you're going to outsource customer service. Even then, the less your customers need to contact you, the better.

Your product shouldn't be a service, unless it's a service you're able to automate. For instance, if you're selling information and have to physically teach each individual who signs up for your program, you won't be able to scale it. If you can turn your course into a web series that students are able to purchase and view at their own pace, then you're able to create the program once and sell it an infinite number of times.

Always be thinking about scalability. If you're doing something today that you'll have to do again tomorrow, try changing your model.

This book is actually the first time in years I've violated the rules of automation and scalability. Under normal circumstances, if I needed sixty thousand words of content, I'd pay a few people on the other side of the world to put it all together and check back in a week. Instead, I'm actually writing this myself. While I enjoy writing and helping others, I can't help but think about the inefficiency of this method.

GETTING CUSTOMERS

"Half the money I spend on advertising is wasted; the trouble is I don't know which half."
—Marketing pioneer John Wanamaker

There was a time when marketers could only guess how well their individual marketing campaigns were doing. If you put up one billboard and your sales went up 50 percent, it's not hard to track where the increase came from. If you put up fifty billboards, run radio spots, and take out ads in all the local papers, it's going to be hard to guess which advertisements are helping you and which ones are draining your wallet.

Marketing also used to require a lot of work. Every time my dad wanted to promote his restaurant, the whole family would have to sit down in the living room and stuff envelopes for hours so he could mail out coupons to potential customers.

With online marketing, I can build a list of people I want to market to, set a price I'm willing to pay per visitor, and let the campaign run indefinitely while I work on other things. There are marketing campaigns I set up seven years ago that I haven't had to touch since, and they still bring in money.

In thirty seconds, I can get a report that tells me exactly how many sales I've gotten from each ad placement, how many people saw a particular ad, how many people clicked on it, and the average amount of time they spent on my website. Online marketing has changed advertising from a guessing game to a science. It's also never been easier to create, manage, and automate marketing campaigns.

If you're going to advertise your company online, you'll need to know the major marketing channels to use. Every large, successful e-commerce site uses all or most of these channels to create customers and make money.

PAID SEARCH

I talk about paid search a lot because it's the best way to drive substantial traffic and test new ideas quickly. It's also one of the easiest channels to automate once you've found a product that works.

A paid-search campaign can be built in a couple hours, can be funded with a small budget, and the results are almost instant. If something isn't working, adjustments can be made quickly.

If you're unfamiliar with paid search, it works like this:

Bob opens his laptop, goes to Google.com and types in the search phrase "buy a Toyota."

Google will show Bob a list of results it believes are relevant. Above these results are advertisements from local car dealerships and national chains.

They look a lot like the natural results. If Bob doesn't see the tiny green square that says "ad," he might not realize these companies are paying to be at the top of the page.

Bob clicks on the top result (like most people), which is an ad that takes him to the website of a local Toyota dealership. Google charges the dealership a couple bucks for the click. Bob fills out his contact information, gets a call from a salesman, and eventually buys a new car. The dealership makes a $30,000 sale, and all it cost was a couple dollars to Google for sending the customer. (Side note: Google is the king of the middleman game. By positioning themselves between consumers and—well, everything—they are able to take a cut of transactions from every industry under the sun.)

Paid search is great for advertisers because they can chose to only show their ads when someone has already expressed interest in their product. You don't have to guess with paid search—it's not like a billboard where most of the people who see your ad have no interest in what you're selling.

Because you can build your paid-search account so that only people who are actually interested in what you have to sell will ever see your ads, you don't have to waste money marketing to people outside your target audience. If the product you pick is "evergreen" (not seasonal, like Halloween costumes or income tax filing), you can set up many of your ads to run indefinitely without any additional work. Even seasonal products don't require much management if you set them up correctly. For instance, if you're paying to show an ad on the words "Halloween costumes" that sends people to your costume store, it may make sense to leave the ad up all year. The only people who will see it are the ones who are in the market for Halloween costumes, and if they want to buy one from you in February, who are you to say no?

The overwhelming majority of paid-search traffic can be accessed through two companies, Google and Microsoft.

Google AdWords

For a while, I was solo managing one of the largest Google AdWords accounts in the world. (Remember, all my formal training came from a For Dummies book.) Using other people's money, I spent $3 million a month learning how to create customers with paid search.

Since my commute to the office could take almost ninety minutes, I got in the habit of getting up early and doing some work before I left. One morning when I was still relatively new to AdWords, I clicked on the wrong check box in an ad campaign. I didn't notice my mistake, and in the time it took me to drive to the office, more than $10,000 had been wasted.

With such a large budget, the mistake was easily averaged in for the month, but I did learn a valuable lesson about using such a powerful platform with as much traffic as Google. Always remember that you can do a lot of damage very quickly if you're not careful.

The basic principles of AdWords are easy. When you first create an account, you won't have access to many advanced options, but you will be able to create basic advertising campaigns.

As an example, let's say I've built a website to sell Halloween costumes. After creating an account and entering my billing info, I'd create a campaign and call it "Super Hero Costumes."

A campaign can contain any number of ad groups (as of this writing, the max number of ad groups per campaign is twenty thousand). Ad groups are where you group together similar keywords, so for my Super Hero Costumes campaign I'd create a few ad groups and name them things like:

Superman Costumes
Wonder Woman Costumes
Batman Costumes

Inside the "Superman Costumes" ad group, I'd create an ad to take people to a landing page where they can buy a child's or adult's Superman costume. Then I'd use Google's keyword tool to come up with the search terms I'd want my ad to show up for. My keyword list would look something like this:

Superman costume
Superman outfit
Superman costume for kids
Superman suit
Adult Superman costume

Make the list as long as you can. Don't limit yourself as long as the keywords are relevant. It's easier to make money if you bid lightly on a lot of keywords than if you bid for top position on one or two. For instance, trying to be the top ad for "Superman costume" will cost you a lot more per click than being the third ad on "Superman costume," "Superman outfit," and "adult Superman costume," and you'll end up with more overall traffic if your keyword list is fully fleshed out. Again, it's important that the keywords are relevant—"Superman Halloween" is a good keyword; "Superman comic" is not.

Later, if the ad for this group gets a lot of clicks, I'll probably split it into two separate ad groups, one for kids and one for adults. For now, I want to get the ad up and running and start testing traffic.

Make sure to write a compelling ad that will make potential customers notice and click. It's hard to overstate the importance of click-through rates. The number of times your ad is clicked versus the number of times it's shown will likely determine the success or failure of your ad campaign. Click-through rates are the largest factor in the formula Google uses to determine the *quality score* of your keywords and ads.

Think of quality score as a multiplier for your bid. When you enter your keywords, you also tell Google the maximum you're willing to pay when someone does a search for the phrase and clicks on your ad. Google's algorithm then takes your bid and compares it against other advertisers to decide the order your ads will show on the results page. The higher bid doesn't always win—a high-quality score can make a $1 keyword bid as effective as a $5 bid if your competitor's ad has a low quality score.

Google wants to make money. If advertiser A's ad is clicked on twice as much as advertiser B's, Google will show advertiser A's ad higher in the search results and charge the advertiser less per click, because the increase in clicks makes Google more money overall. Advertiser B will have to pay more for less traffic.

To save on costs, some people suggest writing text ads that discourage all but the most likely buyers. The problem with this is that by killing your click-through rate you also kill your quality score, forcing you to pay even more for those qualified customers.

Ironically, there have been several times where paying for the extra, unproductive traffic increased my quality score enough that I saved money overall. If a particular keyword is bringing in some customers but also a lot of junk traffic, try lowering your bid until it's profitable. You could also try offering more services or purchase options to turn a higher percentage of those browsers into buyers.

Here are some other tips for success with AdWords that I've picked up over the years:

Don't try to "own" a keyword.

A lot of people will find the biggest keyword for their industry and decide "success" means always being at the top of the page for that keyword. They'll overbid and waste a ton of money.

Instead of trying to be at the top of the page for a small number of keywords, try to get your ad to at least show somewhere on the page for all relevant searches. You'll get more customers at a lower cost if you cast a wider net. Fighting for the top spot while ignoring the long tail is how a lot of people lose money with paid search.

It's a numbers game.

There's a simple equation to paid search. If you pay less per visitor than you make per visitor, you will make money. Manage your bids, improve your quality scores, and tweak your landing pages and sales funnel to squeeze out more orders.

Take advantage of ad extensions.

Whether it's a phone number, site links, or business address, ad extensions increase the amount of space your ads take up on the results page. Larger ads means they're more likely to be clicked, which means a higher quality score and lower cost per click. Add every appropriate extension to all of your ads.

Beware expanded broad match.

Google changed their keyword matching algorithm a while back to allow them to show ads more often and make the company more money. Unless you tell Google to only show your ad when a user types in one of your keywords exactly, Google will look for keywords similar to the ones in your account and display your ad to users searching for those as well. Unfortunately, the algorithm is overly aggressive and will often show your ad for completely unrelated searches.

Run a keyword search report every few days.

Currently this is under the "Keywords" tab in AdWords. Click on the "Search Terms" button to see the actual words people typed into the Google search bar that made your ad show up. The first time you run it, you'll see some crazy stuff. One of the more awkward conversations I had with my boss was having to explain how much of the money we'd spent bidding on the words "cell phones" was actually used to show our ad to people searching for "phone sex."

Find all the terms that are unrelated to your project and add them to the negative keyword list. This prevents Google from showing your ad when someone types in a keyword you don't want to show your ad for. Do this every few days. It will save you a ton of money.

Let profitability determine your budget.

Setting budget caps in AdWords is very important while you're still learning, but once you're able to consistently hit your cost-per-sale metric, you should be spending as much as possible while remaining profitable. If spending $1,000 a day gets me $300 in profit and spending $10,000 a day gets me $3,000, I want to spend $10,000 every day. Don't artificially cap your profits. Just make sure you know what you're doing before raising your daily budgets too high. I set my daily caps high enough so I won't ever hit them on a normal day but low enough so if I make a mistake (like clicking the wrong check box early in the morning), things won't get too far out of hand before Google shuts off the campaign.

Bing Ads (Microsoft)

The first time you log into your Bing ads account, you'll probably experience some déjà vu. You may think you've logged into your Google AdWords account but all of your campaigns are missing. Bing hasn't been much of an innovator in the paid-search space, choosing instead to copy more or less everything Google does.

Many people ignore Bing because it's not the eight-hundred-pound gorilla that Google is. You can profit from this because that means there's usually less competition.

If you've already got a Google account built, it's a no-brainer to also create a Bing ads account. Not only does it give you additional traffic, but Microsoft has made it as easy as possible to copy your entire Google account into a new Bing account so you don't have to worry about doubling the work. Just put in your billing info and you're ready to go.

Yet another reason paid search is my favorite method of advertising is because it's one of the few places where it's possible to make repeated large purchases with a credit card. Google and Bing have helped me rack up millions of airline miles over the years.

DISPLAY ADVERTISING

Display advertising refers to the text and banner ads you see on almost every website. These ads are not as targeted as paid search since users aren't typing in exactly what they're looking for before an ad is shown. Still, the type of site can be a good indicator of a visitor's intent—a blog about mountain biking is probably a good place to serve an ad for new mountain bikes. Large companies like Google track web users' movements across the web and are able to show ads to people whose behavior matches the most likely customers of

Google's advertisers. Ever notice how you'll see tons of jewelry ads for weeks after visiting a single online jewelry store? If you browse an advertiser's website, Google is also able to track you while you visit other websites and show you ads for the original advertiser.

As someone who uses the internet, I find this disturbing. As an advertiser, I'm excited by the marketing opportunities this creepy intrusiveness can provide.

One of the quickest and easiest ways to get into display advertising is through Google's content network. Millions of websites participate in this network, and Google can reasonably target your ads to show on the sites your customers are most likely to visit.

These ads can be bought through Google AdWords, the same as paid-search ads. If you're just starting with AdWords, I'd suggest turning off the content network until you're ready to focus on display advertising.

There are plenty of other companies that will sell you display ad space, but be careful with the more off-brand content networks. They can have very sleazy sites in their network that will either deliver fake clicks (that you have to pay for) or contain websites you wouldn't want your ads on. Personally, I'm not too picky about where my ads show as long as they're making money, but if I've got a partnership going with a big company, it might cause issues if they see an ad for their product in an unsavory corner of the web. (Of course, one might wonder how they found the ad.)

The more niche your product, the more focus you'll need to put into targeting your display ads. Mass-market products can get away with large, untargeted display ad buys, but if you're targeting a small demographic, you may need to skip the networks and approach the owners of relevant websites directly about display advertising deals. The upside is you remove a middleman, which should lower the ad price. It does add a considerable amount of work.

Due to the massive inventory of available display advertising space, this channel can easily end up as your largest order generator or your biggest money loser. I like display almost as much as paid search because, once you find a network or collection of websites that work for you, display advertising requires relatively little effort to maintain.

E-MAIL MARKETING

E-mail marketing is considered by many advertisers to be the most efficient marketing channel, though it's effectiveness has decreased over the years. While there are costs involved, the price per customer is usually much lower than paid channels.

There are two kinds of e-mail marketing. The first kind involves buying or renting an existing e-mail list, then sending your offer to everyone on it. This is the fastest way to get into e-mail marketing and can provide you with millions of potential customers instantly!

Do not do this. Ever.

Most of the e-mail addresses will be fakes. Even the legit addresses will be worthless, since the list has likely been sold over and over and spammed to oblivion. Some of the e-mail addresses are likely to be traps used by e-mail service providers to identify spammers—the only way to acquire these addresses is by buying a spammy e-mail list. When an e-mail service provider like

Gmail sees an e-mail go through to one of these addresses from a marketer, they can immediately tag that marketer as a spammer.

Assuming there are a few legit addresses on the list, these people are still not expecting an e-mail from you and are far more likely to mark any communication from you as spam. When enough people hit the spam button, any e-mails coming from the same domain as your website will be blocked by large e-mail service providers. The third party you use to send the e-mails will likely blacklist you as well. This makes it even harder to do things the right way later.

The right way to use e-mail for marketing is to ask your website visitors to opt in to your e-mail list. In other words, get their permission before you contact them.

Keep in mind that you're changing the call to action by asking for an e-mail sign-up. Usually you'll build a landing page with the sole focus of making a sale, and stopping a customer who's in the decision-making process to ask for an e-mail address can be a turnoff. If a site is annoying about asking for my e-mail address, I'll close the browser window.

If asking for e-mail addresses is affecting your conversion rate negatively, focus first on customers who have already ordered from you and supplied their address. These are the best candidates to remarket to anyway. Come up with reasons to contact them after the sale and offer related products.

When done right, asking customers for e-mail addresses at the start of the purchase flow can be a net positive to conversion rate (the percentage of people who eventually buy), even if it extends the average sales cycle a bit.

An e-mail sign-up has a lower resistance threshold—potential customers may not be willing to spend money with you yet but could be open to learning more about your company or product. They may not turn into a customer today, but you'll be able to remarket to them and squeeze out more orders down the road. This has the effect of increasing the return on investment of your other marketing channels.

It's important to give people a reason to sign up for your e-mail list. Usually this is a special offer or content that's only available to e-mail subscribers.

I give out a promo code that's worth up to $50 to anyone who signs up for my e-mail list. This gets me more sign-ups and also increases my conversion rate.

I used to give the promo code away for free, but it makes more sense to use it as an incentive for visitors to join my e-mail list. Not only does it get me another subscriber, but instead of being forgotten when the potential customer leaves my website, the promo code sits in their inbox as a reminder and helps squeeze more sales out of my marketing efforts.

Since I'm selling a mass-market product, I've been able to grow a sizeable list very quickly. My main landing page has a 20 percent e-mail sign-up rate, getting me up to three thousand new e-mail subscribers every day, or roughly a million e-mail sign-ups annually. I can then contact these people whenever I want. Marketing to a million people through paid search would cost several hundred thousand dollars, but I can be in their inbox tomorrow morning for a fraction of the cost.

When your list is big enough, you can rent e-mail space to other companies in your industry. Whenever you send out an offer to your subscribers, you can tack on an extra offer beneath it from a third party who's willing to pay for the spot. Start with businesses that don't compete with you directly, but even putting in an offer from a competitor could be worth it if the price is right. If you don't want to bother making direct deals, you can sell ad space through an exchange service like LiveIntent.

A lot of e-mail marketing can be automated. The first step is to sign up with an e-mail marketing service like MailChimp or Constant Contact. These services help manage your subscriber lists and allow you to schedule automated e-mails.

Once you have an account and start getting subscribers, it's important to create a drip campaign. This is a specific set of e-mails a new subscriber will get from you in the days and weeks after she signs up.

When a user signs up on my travel site, I send them the promo code immediately. A few days later, I e-mail to ask if they've looked into booking a hotel for their trip. A few days after that, I send an e-mail with some car rental deals at the destination they're interested in. If someone books a flight, I'll send an e-mail a couple weeks before their departure with helpful information about carry-on baggage rules and slip in a few affiliate links to online stores where they can purchase new suitcases.

Instead of coming to my website once, then leaving and forgetting all about it, I'm able to stay at the front of a potential traveler's mind as they research and book their trip.

E-mail marketing is a great candidate for outsourcing. While your drip campaign for new subscribers can be automated, you still have to continually create new content as your list ages. Find a reputable e-mail marketing agency and try to work out a cost-per-action deal so you only have to pay for incremental sales generated through your e-mail channel.

AFFILIATES

I talk a lot about becoming an affiliate and selling other people's products, but being on the other side of the arrangement can be just as lucrative. The are many affiliate networks like LinkShare, Commission Junction, and ClickBank to choose from that give you access to thousands of affiliates who are ready to sell for you.

While it's easier to go the affiliate route if you are offering your own product or service, it's still possible to recruit affiliates even if you are selling someone else's product as an affiliate yourself.

I've known some successful entrepreneurs who signed up for an affiliate program, then recruited sub-affiliates to do all the work for them. This might not make much sense on the surface—why would an affiliate work for you for less money when they could go to the source and get a better deal?

If you're able to move enough volume, you can negotiate a higher commission than what a company pays affiliates in a public network. If the deal is sweet enough, you can turn around and match or beat what the company is offering other affiliates. Make sure the company is aware of what you're doing so there are no surprises later.

Why would a business be okay with you beating their affiliate offer? Managing affiliates is a time and resource sink, which I'll get into in a minute. If you're sending them enough business, you may find they'd rather just deal with you than an army of small affiliates.

The good thing about using affiliate networks to sell your product is that you can set a specific cost you're willing to pay for a sale and let the affiliates do the work for you.

On the surface, letting affiliates do the heavy lifting seems like a great way to outsource your marketing efforts. In reality, making sure affiliates are playing by the rules can be a full-time job.

You'll need a constant flow of fresh offers and marketing collateral to keep your affiliates excited, or they'll move on to other products. There will be technical issues, and you'll get an earful from affiliates with zero sales who swear they know a dozen friends and family members who placed an order, and they want their commission.

If there's a way to make money that's blatantly against the terms of your affiliate agreement, you will have affiliates who will do it anyway. Some of the more clever ones won't create new customers, they'll just find ways of selling you your existing customers.

About a year before I quit my job, I noticed traffic to our branded keywords (i.e. searches on Google for the name of our company or website) decrease. This was a problem because our highest margin orders came from our branded keywords. These were people who already knew us and were trying to find us again to make a purchase. For perspective, our average marketing cost for an order was around $60 to $70. The marketing cost for orders that came through on branded keywords was around $5.

Google only lets one ad for a company show at a time. It took a lot of digging, but eventually I discovered that our affiliates were replacing our ads with their own by outbidding us on Google and placing their affiliate tag in the ad's link.

The reason it took awhile to figure out what the affiliates were doing was because every time someone in our office searched for our brand terms, we still saw our own ad, right there at the top of the page.

Google allows you to geotarget your ads—essentially, you can pick and choose which areas of the world to show your ad, from whole countries down to specific neighborhoods. The affiliates were outbidding us everywhere in the country *except* the Washington, DC area, where they told Google not to show their version of our ads.

This isn't the only time I've seen this happen. It's a standard situation with open affiliate networks, and it can cost companies millions of dollars. One option is to only work with proven affiliates you trust instead of opening up your affiliate program and allowing anyone to join. This might cut down on sales, but it also cuts down on the amount of time you'll have to spend policing your affiliates.

For now, test out a few affiliate networks, and if it turns out to be a profitable channel for you, you can always hire an affiliate manager.

SEARCH ENGINE OPTIMIZATION

A lot of search engine optimizers aren't going to like what I have to say about the subject. That's fine; this section isn't for them. If you're a true SEO expert, you don't need my help to make money.

When people pitch me on a new business idea and I hear them say they'll promote it with "SEO," I replace it in my head with "word of mouth," another equally worthless marketing plan. Essentially, both are shorthand for "I'm going to cross my fingers and hope things work out."

For the uninitiated, search engine optimization (SEO) is all about getting search engines like Google, Yahoo!, and Bing to show a listing for your website near the top of the first page of results when users look for something related to your business. For instance, if you're selling flowers, you'd try to get Google to show your website anytime someone types "send roses" in the search bar. Unlike paid search, these listing are free.

SEO is powerful stuff. If you're in an industry where the average cost per click in paid search is $1, and you're getting a thousand clicks a day from your SEO efforts, you're essentially getting $1,000 a day in free advertising.

SEO is an all-or-nothing game. Depending on your industry, getting into the top three listings on Google for your top keywords can be worth millions of dollars a year. Getting to the top of the second page of results is almost worthless. If you become an SEO expert, you can make a ton of money. It's not worth the time if you're just going to dabble in it. It's not a great candidate for outsourcing, either. A lot of firms will sell you SEO services that include getting other sites to link to yours, but without a way to directly measure the impact, it's usually a waste of money.

Like social media marketing, search engine optimization is as much art as it is a science. One of the best ways to succeed at search engine optimization is to create viral content that other websites will link to, giving you tons of traffic organically and moving your website up in the search engine results. Obviously that's easier said than done.

Solid SEO takes time. You'll have to learn how to optimize the elements on your website to make it more appealing to search engine algorithms. You'll need to contact high-quality websites and blogs and get them to link to your site. You'll need to become a trusted source in your industry who people seek out for answers.

In other words, you're going to have waste a whole lot of time better spent dodging tomatoes at La Tomatina, sipping grappa on the Amalfi coast, or diving with sharks in the Caribbean.

If you're just starting out, I'd caution against making SEO a big part of your marketing strategy.

The one exception to this suggestion is if you have a local business—for example, if you're running a maid service in Dayton, Ohio. It's still relatively easy to get good search rankings for those types of websites. In fact, many national businesses will create smaller, local websites just for the purposes of SEO.

I treat SEO like gravy. I've had websites listed in the top results on Google for extremely competitive and profitable keywords for months, only to fall to the second page and watch hundreds of thousands of dollars in yearly income evaporate. It's great money, but you're always just one algorithm change away from bankruptcy.

Meanwhile, all my other marketing channels have remained relatively consistent for years.

I've had some success with search engine optimization, but it's not at the top of my marketing list because there's no way to automate it. Outsourcing it can be problematic; the results are hard to measure and can take months or years to realize, and there's always potential for damage by an unscrupulous agency. I ranked on the front page for several high-traffic keywords before hiring a well-known agency to take over. Six months and a few links from sketchy websites about Viagra later, my website was nowhere to be found in Google's search results.

This experience reminded me of a very important truth: anyone who's really good at SEO doesn't need to do it for other people. There are so many ways to make money if you can get solid search engine rankings that anyone talented in this area is almost certainly working for himself.

For the time being, I'd suggest finding an independent SEO specialist to audit your site and give you some advice. Don't pay more than a few hundred bucks. Pay attention to best practices, but if you're not willing to become an expert, your time is better spent on other marketing efforts. Focus on offering value and creating engaging content, but don't depend on organic traffic.

SOCIAL MEDIA

Facebook, Instagram, Pinterest, Twitter, Tumblr, and YouTube are all great places to make money. If you think you can make a living pushing your pyramid scheme on your existing group of friends, though, you'll quickly run out of money and friends. You can't use social media as a true sales channel unless you consistently grow your network of followers, and that's hard to do if you're constantly shoving ads down their throats.

This can be a difficult balance to maintain, which is why many companies don't treat social media as a sales channel. For them, social media is more about branding than sales. It puts a human face on a corporation and gives customers a way to interact with the business outside of the sales cycle.

For the purposes of this book, we don't care about branding. We want direct response channels—in other words, we want to be able to measure how much money we're getting back for the work we put in.

To make money in social media, you'll have to build a sizeable following of new potential customers. Be someone your customers want to engage with. If you want to sell purses, create a fashion blog. If you want to sell yoga lessons, use social media to show your expertise. When I wrote my first fiction novel, I built a large social media following by publishing free short stories on Myspace. (Yes, I know, I'm old and lame.)

One of the major drawbacks to social media is that your account will often turn into a public customer service channel. While this presents a great opportunity to showcase how well you treat your customers when issues arise, it's also resource intensive. Unlike other channels, social media is not a space where you have complete control over the message.

Social media is also difficult to automate, but there are a lot of tools to help manage your accounts. A quick Google search will show you many third-party platforms you can use to schedule posts ahead of time and track results.

Social media may be the most time-intensive form of online marketing. Depending on your personality, it might also be the most fun. I've sunk a lot of time into book promotion on social media, and interacting with readers has been incredibly rewarding, minus the occasional soul-crushing criticism.

Fortunately, social media marketing is not the all-or-nothing marketing channel that SEO is. Many people are able to eke out a living by occasionally posting to their social media accounts. Of course, it doesn't hurt if you're already somewhat famous, or at least an underwear model.

I've just described all the major categories of online marketing. You'll find that some of these marketing channels work better than others, and your product and messaging can have a huge impact on which will work best for you. Still, I recommend using every channel you can so long as you can find ways to manage them that aren't time-consuming. Every marketing channel has low-hanging fruit. Generally it's easier to pick up a few extra orders by adding a new channel than it is to continually try to squeeze more out of an overtapped one.

Learning the full array of online marketing skills will also come in handy if, heaven forbid, your start-up doesn't work out and you need to look for work again. Despite not having a "job" in many years, I'm in a much better position to reenter the job market than I was when I left. Of course, I have no intention of that ever happening, but as I've said, there are no guarantees.

CHOOSING A PRODUCT TO SELL

This problem is one that stumps a lot of people. They want to go into business for themselves, they just can't figure out what they'd actually sell.

I love the show *Shark Tank* on ABC. I enjoy seeing the creative new ideas people come up with and build businesses around. Unfortunately, I think it's given potential entrepreneurs the wrong impression, and many of them now think they can't start a business unless they have an innovative and original idea.

You don't need to come up with something new. You can sell anything. In fact, it's better if you sell something that already exists (or is related to something that already exists) because there's a proven market for it.

That doesn't mean you can't make a lot of money off a great original idea. It does mean you shouldn't sit around and wait for one to strike you.

So what product or service should you sell? Preferably one that doesn't require any effort to duplicate. If it does require manufacturing, let someone else worry about production and inventory through outsourcing. I chose travel for my first business because it meant selling electronic tickets. There's no physical inventory to manage.

Selling information is always a solid choice. Not only is it easy to reproduce and scale, but there are a lot of channels built specifically to sell information. Affiliate networks like ClickBank are a great place to find people who are willing to sell your info products.

There's a lot of debate on how targeted you should get with your audience. A lot of people say go niche. The idea is that it's easier to market to a clearly defined potential customer base. Also, there tends to be less competition in smaller markets. This should make it cheaper to reach your target demographic. Niche companies are also able to charge a premium for their product or service.

If you have a very expensive product, it might make sense to go after a small, targeted market. Otherwise, I say it doesn't matter. The negatives of niche marketing usually outweigh the positives unless you're able to find a particularly ripe opportunity.

I built a site that sells airline tickets. How many adults do you know who have ever bought an airline ticket? My market was literally almost everyone. It was as far away from niche marketing as you can possibly get, and it did very well.

(Before you start spinning up a flight ticket website, I will offer a word of caution. Selling flights worked well when I was starting out, though it's not an industry I'd recommend getting into now. Particularly in the United States, airline consolidation has driven reseller margins down to almost nothing. It's a tough market to get into. The only upside is that it's a bit less competitive for established companies.)

If you start selling a niche product, you'll find that getting targeted traffic to your website is expensive. The cost per eyeball on the front page of CNN is far lower than the cost per eyeball on a smaller website targeted to your specific demographic. Again, if you're selling $2,000 courses, it might be worth it. If you're selling $10 leashes designed for pet lobsters, you're not going to do well.

If you've got a niche product and try to mass market it, you will lose a lot of money. If you've got a mass-market product, though, a lot of marketing channels open up. Untargeted traffic is cheap traffic. I've seen cell phone ads on the front page of Yahoo! (at the time the most visited page in the United States) generate millions of dollars in revenue. Everyone needs a cell phone at some point, and the scattershot approach can actually work when your market is big enough.

If your product is too niche, you severely limit the potential size of your business. It's only worth it if narrowing your focus shrinks the number of competitors faster than the pool of potential customers.

A final reason why I don't like extremely niche products is because my favorite marketing channel is paid search, and for people to search for your product, they have to already know it exists. People are already typing in "buy a cell phone" or "book a flight to Orlando" into Google. Nobody is typing "yoga for pet birds" into the search bar.

If you pick a broader market, your competition has already trained consumers to look for your product. When I was selling cell phones, I didn't need to teach consumers why they needed one. I let Verizon and AT&T do that. I just waited for potential customers to search Google for "mobile phones" or "T-Mobile" and then put a deal in front of them that was better than what the phone carrier was willing to offer. We got to piggyback off of their marketing efforts.

It worked the same way for our competition. Every time we took out a front-page ad on Yahoo.com, the other major online cell phone reseller would see a huge spike in sales. We were spending money to get people interested, and that interest benefited everyone in the industry.

Use other people's money (OPM) and draft off their marketing. That's impossible to do in a small niche.

Some people suggest you need to be an expert in the product you want to sell. These are the same people who will tell you to "stick with what you know." If we all stuck with what we knew, none of us would get very far.

I believe being an expert in a particular industry doesn't matter as much as you'd think it would. If you learn marketing and automation, you can sell anything. I know how to enjoy travel, but even after eight years of running a travel company, I'm still quite ignorant to the inner workings of the travel industry. I've sold scented candles. I've sold Snuggies. I've sold skin tag removers. I really don't know much about any of these products (okay, besides the Snuggies). As a middleman, it doesn't matter. You don't need much beyond a basic understanding of the product.

Don't believe me? Think about how most marketing agencies work. They don't pick a single industry and refuse to work with anyone outside of it. A good marketing agency can promote any product because they're experts at sales and marketing. The product isn't relevant.

It's important to develop this ability. Don't sell what you know; sell what works.

I worked backward. I decided how I was going to promote my business (mostly paid search, with some search engine optimization and e-mail marketing) and then looked for a product or service that would work for those channels.

After narrowing it down to a few potential industries, I used sites like Alexa.com to see how much traffic potential competitors were getting. The more traffic, the better, because it meant there was already a market for the product. Then I used Google's keyword tool to find out how much traffic I could get for the product or service using paid search.

Once you've got it down to a couple ideas, test them. Take your first idea and put together a basic website. Sites like Shopify.com make it easy to build an ecommerce website that can handle online transactions. When you've got a website up, buy some traffic. Don't go overboard—depending on the product, I'll shoot for 600 to 700 clicks for an initial test. If visitors are showing zero interest, stop spending money and test another idea.

With online marketing, it's easy to spot a dud before you've lost a lot of money. In the world of physical stores and inventory, people don't know they have a losing idea until they've spent tens or hundreds of thousands of dollars. Don't be afraid to kill an unprofitable idea early.

Sometimes I'll test a new product or use a new marketing channel, and after spending several hundred dollars I'll have no orders to show for it. At that point it's time to reevaluate three things:

The product itself: Is this something people actually want or just something I want to sell them? Are other people having success with this product? Am I priced appropriately?

The landing page: Am I making a compelling offer? Is the site working from a technical standpoint? I've unfortunately seen situations where thousands of dollars were spent on display advertising only to send visitors to an error page.

The marketing channel: There are some scummy ad networks out there. The traffic you're paying for can often turn out to be fake bot traffic from ISPs in Pakistan. Even if the visitors you're paying for are real, the targeting might be so bad that individuals coming to your site will never convert.

For instance, when I first started advertising on mobile devices, I didn't realize that Google would place my ads inside iPhone and Android apps. Clicks on these ads are very often by mistake—and unscrupulous developers try to design their apps to get the most accidental ad clicks possible to increase their revenue.

Mobile content sites are also guilty of this—the ones with article headlines like "You Won't Believe What Happens Next" or "Which Disney Princess Are You?" (I'm Jasmine, FYI) that are stuffed to the gills with ads. It's almost impossible to scroll down the page without accidentally clicking on at least one.

(Side note—while shady, this is actually a brilliant business model. These sites pay very little to content creators to churn out click-bait articles, then rake in advertising dollars from marketers who aren't paying attention to where their ads are being served).

If you do get a sale or two from your test, or you end up with a bunch of e-mail sign-ups, you may have found a winner even if your initial return on investment is negative. Put in the work to build a decent landing page and an optimized ad campaign, then test the idea again. Let your potential customers—not your own preferences—determine how and what you sell.

DON'T LET COMPETITION SCARE YOU

You don't need billion-dollar budgets and focus groups. You don't need to outperform the big guys at every step. All you need are a few small things to differentiate yourself when it's time for a customer to make a decision.

If you have well-entrenched competition, you have a great advantage. You can shamelessly copy them. I'm not talking about trademarks and patents; I'm talking about business practices, product messaging, and positioning.

The guys spending the most on Google ads (the ones who are almost always at the top of the page) are probably the ones making the most money—otherwise the cost of such expensive advertising would have bankrupted them by now. Emulate them as much as you can.

Look at their messaging. This will tell you what they've found to be most important to potential customers. The big guys have spent a lot of time and money testing their landing pages to see what works. Save yourself both the time and the money and learn from their tests. Obviously you can't just copy and paste their landing pages onto your website, but borrow liberally (without infringing on copyright or trademarks).

Try to beat them on one value proposition. Maybe you'll offer free shipping if they don't. Maybe your product will come with a guarantee and a better return policy. When customers can compare offerings side by side, just being a couple cents cheaper can make a huge difference.

Paid search is a fairly efficient market. If other people are making more money than you, they can outbid you and take most of the traffic for a certain set of keywords. When I started out, I knew I had to get the healthiest payout possible per sale to be able to compete. When looking at your business model, make sure your margins allow you go head-to-head with the competition—if they're making $50 in revenue per sale and you're making $15, you're going to have a hard time buying up web traffic. Cut out other middlemen, increase the ad revenue on your site, or get higher affiliate payouts—whatever it takes to give you more margin to use in the fight for traffic.

On the ad creative side, you have to be just a little bit smarter than the other advertisers. Most ad platforms reward you for ads that are more relevant to their users. Often they'll sell you ad space at a lower cost if they believe showing your ads is better for their users and will make them more money in the long run.

You also need to make sure your landing page is better at turning visitors into customers. Always be testing. Tweak the offer and messaging to squeeze out more orders than your competition can with same number of visitors.

It doesn't take much. If you execute even slightly better than your competitors, you can take the lion's share of their traffic and eat their lunch—from the beach in Positano, Italy, while your business runs itself.

AUTOMATE—THEN AUTOMATE MORE

Getting the deals in place to handle fulfilment and building out your advertising campaigns are the most work-intensive pieces of starting a new online business.

The good news is that once everything is up and running the hard part is over. If you've built automation into your company from the ground up, it should be able to run without any additional input from you. After you've told Google what keywords you want to bid on and how much you're willing to pay, you can leave your campaigns on indefinitely.

Traffic comes in. Orders are placed. They're automatically sent to a third party for fulfilment. You get your cut. You take another sip of your margarita.

All day, every day.

That's the ideal situation, of course. In reality, you're going to run into unexpected issues, especially early on. You'll need to keep an eye on your marketing to make sure you're not spending more than you're bringing in. You may think of new keywords to bid on. Maybe you'll come up with some product upsells to tack on to your existing offers.

You may find you can't afford your marketing costs with your existing margins. Go back and renegotiate deals. Be honest. Give your suppliers a reasonable projection of the business you can send them if they work with you on the money side and let them know the orders will dry up if they can't be flexible.

With the big stuff out of the way, you can focus on automating your daily routines and cutting down on the amount of wasted time. The best place to start is eliminating the information overload you'll face as the new CEO, CFO, COO, CMO, and every other important position in your new company.

I spent a lot of time early on pouring over useless information. I'd check my ad spending every ten minutes, answer every unsolicited e-mail, and pour through dozens of unhelpful reports. It was a huge waste of time.

I streamlined the information I received and set up automated alerts so I don't have to manually check everything all the time. If my daily marketing spend goes above a certain threshold, or if Google doesn't approve one of my ads, I get a notification. All these alerts go to my phone. I travel with my laptop, but as long as nothing breaks, it stays in the suitcase.

Every morning I get reports sent to me with a breakdown of the previous day's marketing spend and revenue generated. The reports are designed to let me see very quickly if there's an issue. I check my e-mail from my phone, and if everything is going well, I'm free to work on my next project.

If you're coming from an office environment, you know how easily your day can fill up with worthless meetings, phone calls, and e-mail chains. Be honest— how many hours of your day are spent doing truly productive work? Think about how much of your workweek in an office is just wasted time. This is your opportunity to get all of that time back. You're in charge now.

If you get all your work done by ten a.m., you don't have to pretend to be busy for the next seven hours. You can go rent a Jet Ski. You've worked hard for that flexibility. Don't let anyone steal it from you.

People will try.

Account managers will come up with any excuse to schedule a conference call. Their job is to take up your time. Their two main goals are to show their bosses that they're actually working by contacting you all time and to find ways to make more money off of you.

Tell them you're too busy for a call but to send you a summary e-mail. There's almost nothing that can't be explained in a two-paragraph e-mail message.

Don't be rude. You don't want them to dislike you since you'll likely need their help at some point. You just want them to stop bothering you.

Vendors will contact you over minor issues. Ignore them. If you have to, set up a permanent out-of-office auto-response in all of your e-mail accounts.

Eventually everyone you do business will learn not to bother you with time-consuming trivialities. Just make sure you're available to quickly respond when serious issues arise.

Go through every daily process and find a way to automate or outsource it. Bill paying is an easy one to consolidate and automate. I put everything on a credit card because it gives me cash back, lets me pay for everything on one bill, and helps with cash flow by giving me some extra time to pay (though I never keep a balance).

When I need to review my expenses, everything is in one place. American Express's online reporting can break down my annual spend by category and vendor. This is a big help when it comes time to file taxes.

I save time by having an incredibly small IT footprint. I pay $600 a month in IT costs to run a website that gets millions of visitors. If I need something changed on the site, I send an e-mail to India, and the work is done by the time I get up in the morning. There are no priority meetings, no "roadmapping," and no arguing about resources or timetables. It just gets done.

For e-mail marketing, I'd suggest hiring someone on commission. Pay them on orders generated. Same goes for social media. Those channels are time hogs, but it doesn't make sense to hire someone to manage them full-time for $50,000 or more a year plus benefits when you're starting out.

When you meet with other companies, you'll walk away with "next steps" or "action items." It's basically a to-do list. Push as many of these to their side as possible, even if it seems like the work should be done by you. Explain that you have limited resources and the project will move along faster if they do it on their end.

If you're spending enough money with Google to have an account rep, they'll often have suggestions to improve your AdWords account. If you agree with their suggestions, ask if they'll do the work to implement them.

If you're an affiliate of a larger company, ask if their programmers and creative team can give your website a professional redesign. A better website for you means more sales for them.

Use the resources of large corporations to save yourself time and money. I've relied on partner companies to:

Build me a free, modern e-commerce site
Create, run, and operate the entire customer payment and fulfilment process
Hire and pay for customer service representatives
Monitor my advertising channels and alert me to any issues

If you continue to automate and remove all unnecessary work, you'll eventually hit your stride. The companies I work with are usually shocked to find out I'm the only full-time employee of my company.

Think of it this way. For every job you automate in your new business, you're paying yourself another salary and giving yourself more time to focus on growing your business—or enjoying the benefits of being your own boss.

WHY THIS IS THE BEST BUSINESS MODEL

"I'm in the empire business."
—Walter White

After I offloaded all my work, I had an excessive amount of time to either spend on leisure activities or build out another business. I can choose to do as much or as little work as I want, but when I choose to work, my efforts go toward creating new revenue streams, not simply maintaining what I already have.

It's not laziness. It's *choice creation*.

You don't have the freedom to continue growing personally or professionally if you're always in maintenance mode.

I've automated my businesses to the point where I don't even need my laptop anymore. When I need to get away or work on another project, I use my cell phone every so often to make sure everything is still up and running.

I can start another business with the free time I've gotten back. I can take the same automated business model and recreate it in another industry. Once it's up and running, I can create another and another.

I firmly believe the best business model is one that can continuously make money for you without any additional effort. Every hour you spend maintaining your business is an hour spent not growing.

One word of caution: If you want to build a billion-dollar business, the automated, low-effort model is probably not the path to go down. Not to say it's impossible for a completely automated business to hit that mark, but it's a harder sell to potential buyers when all of the company's assets only exist on your cell phone.

If you're smarter than everyone else, ready to work harder than everyone else, and willing to take more risk than anyone else, then by all means try to make the next Uber.

If you want a steady income and the ability to enjoy your money and free time, work on building an automated business.

Once you have it up and running, it can fund other ventures. It can fund your innovative, billion-dollar, industry-changing idea. You'll be in a better position to give it your all because you'll have cash flow and won't be worried about losing your house or how you're going to feed your kids.

It gave me the free time to write a book. Most people who aren't full-time authors have to squeeze in their writing time early in the morning or before they go to bed. I'm writing this paragraph in the middle of the day between scuba lessons.

A FEW THINGS TO KEEP IN MIND

Resist the urge to go all in.

When you get things off the ground and start to make profit on paper, don't quit your job and max out your credit cards. Overleveraging is a dangerous game, and it's easy to end up cash poor. Even if you're profitable, you might not be able to pay your bills.

There's also the very real danger that a company or individual you work with could go bankrupt. If they provide a large chunk of your income, your paper profits could disappear. Overleveraging is how entrepreneurs lose their homes.

Competition isn't always the enemy.

Having another company out there that does the same thing you do means you always have at least one potentially large customer. Bringing in more business than you can handle? Sell it to your competitor. Companies buy and sell leads from each other every day.

A lot of my revenue comes from competitors. I'm always thrilled to take their money.

Maybe your competition offers an additional service that you don't. Ask if they'll white label it and allow you to sell their service under your brand.

STOP WITH THE EXCUSES

But I don't have any good business ideas.

I know one guy who retired in his thirties and writes a blog on how he and his family of four live on less than $30,000 a year. On his blog, he has links to cash-back credit cards and other ways for his readers to save money. Of course, he gets advertising revenue from the links. He doesn't make a ton of money, but as his blog will tell you, it's more than enough for his needs.

You don't need a great idea for a business. Do you like skiing? Write a blog about it. Then join REI's affiliate program and sell some skis. Not into skiing? Whatever you're interested in, you can probably find something on Amazon that's related enough to sell to your readers.

Don't let excuses like "I don't have anything to sell" stop you from making money. There are millions of people out there who do have something to sell, and they will pay you to help them.

Join an affiliate network like LinkShare and look through the offers until something jumps out at you. Try selling that product. If it doesn't work out, pick another one. Do some more testing. Experiment and learn until you've got a product that works for you and the marketing knowledge to sell it.

I'm scared to quit my job.

This is an easy one. You don't have to. In fact, it's better if you keep your job while you start your first business. Just make sure to do it on your own time.

Check your noncompete clause as well as any paperwork you may have signed regarding intellectual property. While neither is usually an issue, it's best if the industry you get into isn't directly related to your current day job.

Once you get a taste of being your own boss, it can be difficult to drag yourself to work every day. Resist the urge to walk into your boss's office and quit when that first check comes in.

I had a friend, Nate, who had a solid marketing job with a software company. His hours were very flexible, which made it easy for him to start a side business. After a couple months of profits, he told me he was ready to quit his job.

I told Nate to stick it out as long as he could. There was no hurry; he should enjoy having two income streams until he had enough money in the bank to weather any downturns in his new business.

He put in his two-week notice the next day.

One week later, he had to dissolve his new company. The single point of failure in his supply chain failed, and he had no way to replace it. He went from two income streams to zero.

Becoming your own boss should improve your financial position, so jumping ship too early is counterproductive. Use the extra income to boost your savings and give yourself an extra cushion for protection should something happen to your new business. When the time is right, pull the trigger.

If you've planned accordingly, far from adding risk, leaving your job to focus on your business can actually give you more stability. You'll learn the tools companies use to make money, which will help your financial future more than any other form of education.

After I quit my job, I had to sink or swim on my own. I was solely responsible for a company that quickly grew to millions of dollars a year in annual revenue. Before I left my job, I had marketing experience. Now I have executive experience. I have business development experience. I have experience in negotiating deals, hiring, accounting, and management. Even if my company went bankrupt tomorrow, all that experience would allow me to get a much better job than I had when I left the workforce. I wouldn't have any of these skills without starting a business.

Building your own company shows ambition and ingenuity, both of which are in demand when businesses look to fill high-paying positions. Not having a job can be the best resume builder. Of course, if all goes well, the only resumes you'll have to think about are from people asking you for work.

CHAPTER 8

THE INTERNET IS STILL THE WILD WEST

I am by no means condoning most of what you read in this chapter.

Most of the people I'll mention are very clever. Some of them, however, are playing a dangerous game. If you try to copy everything in this chapter and end up getting sued—or even wind up in jail (as some of these' people have), don't blame me. I warned you.

Why am I telling you about them, then? Some of the people I'll discuss are complete frauds, but several others used solid, innovative business practices; they just took things a step too far. While a lot of stuff in this chapter may be immoral and possibly illegal, with sufficient tweaking, it can be the start of a legitimate business model. What's important is that these ideas get you thinking.

When you think of young, successful guys in business suits who "work hard and party harder," what industry do you picture?

I'm talking about guys who go to nightclubs and spend thousands of dollars on bottle service, the guys who post selfies on Instagram of themselves on a yacht with their model girlfriend(s).

What profession does this make you think of?

Most people would probably guess I'm talking about investment bankers. The *Wall Street* type. If this was sometime between the 1980s and the crash in 2007, they'd probably be right.

In 2006, the average pay (salary, bonuses, benefits) for an employee at Goldman Sachs was $622,000. That's just the average—many employees made a lot more than that.

There was a lot of shady stuff going on in the stock world back then.

In 2000, an electric, natural gas, and communications company named Enron reported $111 billion in revenue (more than most countries). It was "America's Most Innovative Company" for six years in a row according to *Fortune* magazine.

Turned out it was a little too innovative. Through creative accounting, Enron executives were able to inflate the company's earnings on paper even while it lost millions. They hyped the company's performance while selling hundreds of millions of dollars in stock. A few months later, those shares were worthless.

It was a huge scandal, but only a year later it was topped by WorldCom and the largest accounting fraud in US history—at least until a few years later when a Ponzi scheme led by Bernie Madoff defrauded investors out of $64 billion.

Perhaps you've heard of Jordan Belfort, also known as The Wolf of Wall Street. He was pocketing as much as $50 million a year for himself while scheming the system.

Of course, what these guys did wasn't legal. So much of the profit they generated was based on smoke and mirrors.

That doesn't mean all of the success in the financial sector was fake or stolen, but to the outside observer, the crazy levels of excess we saw were very often a product of unsustainable business practices or, in some cases, outright fraud.

Things changed after 2007. In the space of a year, Goldman Sachs's stock lost more than three-quarters of its value. The company eventually agreed to pay out more than $5 billion for its part in the banking and housing crisis.

Not long after the crash, I remember hearing a Wall Street banker talk about the moment he realized there was a problem. His paycheck had fallen to "only $100,000" a month. Of course, it kept falling, and before long this guy who was used to partying with celebrities had to move back in with his parents.

While it's still possible for some bankers to make a fortune, the average salary of an investment banker has slipped considerably since the glory days. A giant spotlight was pointed at the financial sector. While many people believe not enough has changed since the days before the crash, it is definitely harder to make those obscene levels of money.

So if you're someone looking to acquire wealth on that type of scale, where should you go now?

Where are young, motivated people still making ridiculous sums of money?

Where's the next shady industry with few rules and lots of opportunity?

Turns out it's even easier to make money with the next big thing, and anyone with an internet connection can get involved. You don't even need to pass a Series 7 exam to get started.

PASSING THE TORCH

I had a front-row seat to the economic meltdown of 2007, but it wasn't on Wall Street. I was in an office in Georgetown, an upscale neighborhood in Washington, DC.

It's some of the poshest real estate in the country. The company I was working for had an entire floor overlooking the Potomac River. There were a lot of prominent names on its board of directors, from a former vice presidential candidate to a former CEO of Apple and Pepsi.

We were selling cell phones by the truckload. This was before the iPhone, back when the Razr was the hottest piece of phone tech. Besides their own website, the company also powered the cell phone purchase flow for companies like Amazon and Walmart. If you bought a cell phone before 2008, you probably got it from this company.

The business model was ingenious. At the time, companies like AT&T were paying resellers about $400 for new customers. The company I was working for figured out that you could buy a phone for $200 and give it away for free. The customer got a free phone, the cell phone company got a new customer, and there was $200 profit left over.

When that didn't move sales fast enough, they started tacking on rebates of $50 or $100. At one point, a customer could get a $200 phone for free, plus another $200 in cash back from rebates. In the end, very few people were able to actually redeem those rebates (which led to an investigation by the FCC as well as the attorney general of the District of Columbia).

The thing I most remember about the job was how far I was in over my head. It was my first "grown-up" job, and I was in charge of a very large marketing budget. The company had raised several hundred million dollars from firms like Goldman Sachs and Citigroup, and took on millions more when it went public.

After only a couple weeks on the job, it looked to me like they were trying to spend it all as fast as humanly possible.

It started with the happy hours. There was a bar on the first floor of our building, and it was common for everyone to meet there after work, rack up a couple grand in food and drinks, and have an executive put it on a company card.

I couldn't afford a place near the city, so my commute was an hour or more each way with traffic. Since a taxi was out of the question, I couldn't get as crazy as the rest of my coworkers, but I didn't want to miss out on after-hours networking.

At the end of my first week, I joined the rest of the office at the bar. I was halfway through my first beer, watching a yacht full of partiers pull up to the dock outside, when a coworker elbowed me.

"Check this out," said Matt, a fellow twentysomething employee, holding up his cell phone. It was a picture of an attractive blonde coworker of ours, completely naked. I'd met her for the first time earlier that day.

"This one, too!" he said, scrolling on his phone to a picture of another female coworker, also nude.

A round of shots for everyone at the bar interrupted the slideshow. I passed, citing my long commute home. There were some dirty looks and a couple of shrugs, but it was quickly forgotten as the tequila disappeared down a few dozen thirsty throats.

I excused myself and left the bar. As I walked to my car, I passed Russell. He sat in front of the office every day in his wheelchair holding a cup and asking for change. The sign on his lap said he was a wounded veteran. I had a couple bucks on me, so I gave it to him.

I was new, so I made it a point to be at the office before anyone else. I got in early the next morning to find Matt passed out under his desk. He woke up for a moment, slurred out a few drunken words, and then fell back asleep.

Around lunchtime, I walked to the kitchen to grab a drink and found a couple VPs playing foosball. A distinguished-looking older man was sitting at the counter drinking a soda. We had a polite conversation. I assumed he was an executive or member of the board. I found out later he was the CEO's driver. We were bleeding millions of dollars a month, and our CEO had a chauffeur.

I noticed a few more VPs coming out of the nearby elevator. They were returning from lunch. It was pouring outside, but they looked mostly dry.

"I can't believe we took a cab from Clyde's," I overheard one of them say.

I couldn't believe it, either. Clyde's was exactly one block from our office.

Money was draining out of the company at an astounding rate. It wasn't just perks. The company was spending millions of dollars a month on advertising. They were addicted to revenue. We were one of the largest accounts at Google, AOL, Yahoo!, and MSN.

A lot of the money was being spent on paid-search advertising, so when anyone went to Google and typed in "cell phones," the first result would be our company's website. At some point before I started working there, the higher-ups realized Google would usually show ads for eight websites when someone searched for those keywords, so they went and made seven copies of our website, created seven different Google accounts, and bought all the ad space.

Still, it wasn't enough.

After getting back to my desk, the CEO walked up, his closed umbrella still dripping from the rain. He flipped it over and held it like a golf club.

"I want you to bid on more keywords," he told me.

"We're already bidding on almost a million cell phone–related words," I told him. It was true—you'd be surprised how many related terms and misspellings there are in any industry. "I don't think there are any more."

He nodded in agreement, then pretended to swing at an imaginary golf ball.

"I want you to bid on all the keywords."

"All the…" I didn't understand. Was he asking me to bid on every word in the English language?

"All the keywords. If someone searches for 'red balloons,' I want them to see our cell phone ad."

He was. He wanted me to advertise on *all the words*. No matter what someone typed into Google, he wanted our ad at the top of the page. We'd be paying to show up on billions of unrelated searches every day.

"How much do you think that would cost?" he asked.

"I honestly have no idea." *All the money*, I thought to myself.

We never found out. The company filed for bankruptcy a few weeks later. All that money—hundreds of millions of dollars—was gone. In fact, more than that was gone, since the company owed millions of dollars to affiliates and advertising partners.

I came to work one morning to see a very large, armed security guard standing by the receptionist. He was there for two reasons: The first, of course, was that a lot of people had just lost a lot of money and weren't happy about it. Second, it was layoff day.

I watched from my cubicle that afternoon as a steady stream of crying faces passed by on their way out of the office. I'd gotten used to the cussing, but I was surprised when I heard a few coworkers giggling in the next cubicle.

I popped my head over the wall to find out what was so amusing. They let me in on the secret.

Apparently, in a last act of defiance, a disgruntled female employee had defecated on the floor of the lady's room.

I left early that day, just in time to see Russell dust off his legs and stand up. He gave me a nod and then proceeded to push his wheelchair up the hill away from the river.

A lot of people lost a lot of money with that start-up. Yet, somehow, a few people were able to walk away very wealthy. Early investors who cashed out when the company went public hit it big. I was shocked that people were able to make so much money on a company that lost millions.

My curiosity piqued, I spent a few years looking into other internet start-ups. I found many of them followed a common formula:

Raise a bunch of money.
Grow revenue or adoption by absurd amounts no matter the cost.
Cash out and leave someone else holding the bag.

This model is still around today. People see the next big thing and want a piece of it, but they're usually too late. These companies are not built on profit—they're built around a scheme involving rapid growth on paper that allows investors to dump their shares on an excited public and rake in a bunch of money, even if the company itself never makes a dime.

All the initial investment is spent "buying" revenue to excite new investors, letting the old ones cash out. It's a legal Ponzi scheme.

To be fair, if you're buying into one of these companies, you're probably not doing your homework. Yet many are duped into these types of investments every day. I'd discovered one way of making a lot of money, but not one I wanted to participate in.

This time in my life was the last lesson I needed to finally accept that there are no guarantees when it comes to money. You can work your heart out for a company for decades only to come to work one morning and find all the doors locked. You can put your life savings in "safe" investments only to lose it all.

You may have heard that diversifying is one of the best things you can do when you invest, and there's a good reason behind it. No one can guarantee that any particular decision regarding money won't end disastrously. The more money you have in different areas, the more protection you have against bad luck.

The same strategy applies to earning money. The safest thing you can do is learn how to make a lot of it, ideally from multiple sources. Money is like insurance against poverty. You can't guarantee you'll never be poor, but the more money you're able to make (and hold on to), the stronger your insurance policy.

A rich person's bad financial day is better than a poor person's bad financial day.

This lesson taught me that the "risks" my parents took in starting their own business were actually far more reasonable than the risk of going to a mediocre job every day, hoping that you'd still be employed tomorrow.

I decided that being rich and working for myself was the least risky path. The internet seemed like a great place to make it happen.

Many people fantasize about winning the lottery, then marching into their boss's office to quit on the spot. That's what it felt like the day I stopped working for other people.

My initial investment of $6,000 (and a lot of time) into my online business was already bringing in $30,000 a month with no additional work on my part. The company I was working for at the time had just trimmed my bonuses, and I wasn't sure how much longer they'd be in business.

The business I built was completely automated, so I could have kept my job and let the cash machine keep making money, but I wanted to make it grow.

Also, after working past midnight every night to get the business off the ground, I wanted some downtime.

Many of my friends thought I was crazy to give up my day job. Some of the coworkers I was close to asked me why I would give up a safe paycheck. Unfortunately, those same coworkers were still at the company when it went under and, as far as I know, still haven't been paid for their last several weeks of work.

The summer after I quit, I had my first month with over $100,000 in profit.

I'd left the "safe" world behind and stepped into a financial world I never knew existed. I came into contact with many other entrepreneurs who worked from home, made their own schedules, traveled when they wanted to, and made six- or seven-figure salaries.

I always envied my bosses who made more money than I did. Now I made the same or more, and, unlike them, I had the time to enjoy it.

SKEPTICISM

I'm sure you've seen advertisements that promise six-figure salaries for very little work. You already know these are almost all scams. It's good to be skeptical, and I'll tell you why.

The truth is, those kind of "jobs" actually exist, but you're not likely to learn about them from someone running those ads.

It's because those kinds of opportunities require not only being in the right place at the right time but enough knowledge to take advantage of the situation.

These specific opportunities come and go—and if you find one, you definitely don't tell others about it. You ride it for as long as you can, make as much money as you can from it, and then look for the next opportunity.

Let me put it this way: If there was a tree in your backyard that grew money, would you tell people about it or would you just grab all the money yourself?

Sometimes, though, people can be persuaded to give up their secrets. I've managed to pry quite a bit of info out of internet entrepreneurs in the past few years, often over drinks.

I recently met a twenty-three-year-old who was making several million dollars a year. We were barhopping on "Dirty Sixth" in downtown Austin, and after several drinks, he told me how he makes more in a year at twenty-three than most people make in their entire life.

He sells a product (I won't name it, for several reasons) that he advertises on Facebook. My understanding is that Facebook has banned advertisement of this particular product because several advertisers have made false or questionable claims about it. Anytime they find an advertiser promoting it, they ban that advertiser's account.

In a way, they did him a favor by getting rid of his competition. He found a company in China that will make thousands of Facebook advertising accounts from different IP addresses, allowing him to put up ads faster than Facebook can ban the accounts.

"Don't you need a credit card for each account?" I asked.

He pulled out his phone and showed me a picture of his work desk. It was covered in what looked like boxes for business cards.

"Prepaid debit cards. Thousands of them," he said with a smile.

"Wow," I replied before downing another $1 shot of tequila (which are almost a requirement on Dirty Sixth). "It's like you're a drug dealer."

"I know!" he said, beaming.

There's a rush that comes with finding loopholes in the system. Breaking the rules and making tons of cash makes some people feel like the online version of *Scarface*'s Tony Montana.

Again, this is where I remind you that I make no claims to the legality or overall consequences of what I'm divulging here. I believe it's important to paint an accurate picture and that this information is valuable to anyone getting involved in online business. A lot of my best ideas came from learning about questionable business practices and figuring out how to turn them into aboveboard, legit businesses. It's a great way to get you thinking outside the box.

It's also important to know what you're up against.

THE EARLY DAYS

Finding loopholes used to be easy. In the first decade of this millennium, online marketing was a completely untamed frontier.

There were no e-mail spam filters. There was no CAN-SPAM Act. E-mail marketing was as simple as buying a list of a few million names and sending out ads for Viagra 24-7.

Getting your website to the top of Google's search results was as simple as posting links on a bunch of forums and loading up a page with a lot of related keywords. Thousands of directory websites sold listings—if you were in a high-profit industry and could afford to get listed on all of them, you were almost guaranteed top spots across every search engine.

Press releases, which were distributed across vast online networks, could be filled with links and spam and had very little editorial oversight.

In one instance, a press release went out about Google's acquisition of a small Wi-Fi company for $400 million. The media ate it up. The company's stock (worth less than a penny each) soared.

The problem was that the press release was a fake. Somewhere in the world, an unscrupulous day trader was making a killing on the fictitious buyout story.

Search engine optimization was so simple that activists were able to change Google's search results for the term "miserable failure" so that a biography of then-President George W. Bush was at the top of the page.

It was still relatively easy in 2006 when I was able to rank my first book's website at the top of Google search results for "self-published author."

Social media marketing was a breeze before big brands caught on. In the days of Myspace, it was a great, honest way to connect with people. My first book was a fiction novel, so I made a Myspace account and put up short stories for anyone who followed me to read for free.

My account grew to over thirty thousand followers. In today's social media environment, where corporations and celebrities can have tens of millions of followers, that's peanuts. The level of engagement and enthusiasm from each follower, though, was something that could never be matched in today's cynical, advertisement-heavy setting. Social media was the perfect place to advertise precisely because people weren't expecting advertising.

Those thirty thousand followers were enough to put me on the best-selling list for fantasy novels on Amazon.

As we've all heard, nothing good lasts forever.

THESE DAYS

Several of the early methods of online money-making still exist, just in a different form.

The low-hanging fruit may be gone, but there are still tons of ways to make money online. While it's gotten harder to rank higher on search engines for competitive keywords like "credit cards" or "car dealership," it's not too difficult to affect the search rankings of specific people or companies.

One new way of making money that's sprung up in the last few years is reputation management. For a fee, a reputation manager will work to remove any negative articles that may show up when someone searches for you or your company on the internet. They'll also make sure that positive stories show up near the top of the results. The reputation manager charges a hefty premium, sometimes $10,000 a month or more. For some companies, the cost is worth it to protect their brand image.

On the flip side, *negative* reputation managers are modern-day corporate assassins. For a price, they'll bombard your competitors with negative reviews, set up "consumer interest" websites warning people away from your competitors' products, and make sure every bad article of press about them is the first thing people see when searching for the company on Google.

Then there's the nuclear option—getting your competition removed from Google outright.

Google and Bing have a lot of rules regarding SEO that companies have to follow or risk being banned from their search results. A lot of these rules apply to things that happen outside of your own website. For instance, paying other websites to link to yours (if it's not marked as an ad) is a big no-no. Essentially, Google believes you're trying to trick its algorithms into thinking your website is more popular than it really is, and they take a hard stance against this kind of practice.

Someone practicing negative SEO would target a competitor's website and buy a whole bunch of cheap links on other websites. They would point all these links to the competitor's site. Google and Bing have no way of knowing who's paying for the links, so there's a good chance they'll penalize the competitor's website.

With the competitor out of the way in the search results, your own site is free to move up.

Obviously, this is pretty terrible thing to do. This is also why you should be careful if you ever have to fire a reputation management company.

AFFILIATE MARKETING

Affiliate marketing is another part of the online world that has evolved considerably. For the unfamiliar (or those who skipped ahead in the book), affiliate marketing is when companies pay third parties to sell their products on commission.

The tools to police affiliates were almost nonexistent in the beginning, and unscrupulous marketers took full advantage of the situation.

One of eBay's early affiliates, Shawn Hogan, managed to pull in almost $30 million in revenue. According to eBay, Hogan used a process known as "cookie stuffing" to place his eBay affiliate code on 650,000 computers, and if anyone using those computers later went to eBay to buy something, he'd get credit. At one point, he was making more than a million dollars a month.

This went on for several years, but it all ended when the FBI raided his apartment in 2013. He was indicted and sentenced to five months in federal prison. eBay sued to recover the affiliate payouts, and they settled out of court.

A sort of cold war has developed between big brands and affiliates. While the big brands love the extra sales, they're now more aware of how easy it is to be ripped off by creative affiliates.

One of the easiest ways for people to take advantage of an affiliate program was through paid-search ads on the company's brand traffic. For instance, an affiliate would join AcmeTshirts.com's affiliate program and put ads up for AcmeTshirts.com on Google whenever someone searched for "AcmeTShirts.com." The person searching on Google was likely already a customer to begin with (which is why they were Googling the website), so all the affiliate was doing was taking credit for the sale.

The bigger brands caught on to this quickly, but it took a long time for small- and medium-size businesses to figure it out. This problem affected every company with an affiliate program.

It led to the creation of an entirely new industry—software to police affiliates. Now you can buy a program that will constantly search Google, Yahoo!, or Bing and alert you when an affiliate is bidding on your brand traffic. The developers of these programs charge a monthly fee and do very well for themselves.

Another trick that worked well in the early days (and is still very much alive) is strategic "domain parking." Ever type the URL of a website incorrectly and get a page with a list of search results? You just helped an online marketer pay his bills.

For strategic domain parking, online marketers would buy misspellings of popular websites, preferably ones related to e-commerce. For instance, someone might buy the domain "AmericanExpres.com" and load the page up with credit card ads. They'd do the same with similar misspellings, so that whenever someone incorrectly types the address for AmericanExpress.com, the marketer gets free traffic and generates ad revenue.

Occasionally the marketers get sued by the brand they were trying to imitate, but a lot of these marketers have thousands if not millions of pages generating clicks and ad revenue every hour. Having to turn over a few pages every so often isn't a big deal to them.

CLICK ARBITRAGE

Domain parking (when done for ad revenue) is a form of *click arbitrage*. If you haven't heard of click arbitrage, let me be the first to introduce you to a whole new way to build wealth with minimal effort.

Click arbitrage is how people retire to the French Riviera and let their bank accounts grow while working on their tans.

Before the internet, generating passive income normally required a hefty amount of capital. Someone looking to make a lot of money for very little work would need to have a lot of money to begin with. They could invest this money in a business or in stocks and live off the returns.

With the advent of the internet and automated tools, there are nearly limitless opportunities to creative passive-income streams that don't require much more than an initial investment of time. I often call this money *automated income*, as it works much differently than traditional passive-income streams. Most of these opportunities involve some form of click arbitrage.

When you're participating in click arbitrage, you're not selling a product. You're selling clicks. You're selling eyeballs and page views. Actually selling the product is someone else's job.

Click arbitrage is, in my opinion, the best business to be in. There are tons of different business models, so you can find what best suits you. Most involve a web presence of some kind and selling ads.

Essentially, click arbitrage is the process of attracting internet users to your website, and then getting them to click on something that makes you more money than the cost to bring the person to your site in the first place.

Online newspapers have been doing this since the nineties. They generate content (news) that brings people to their website, then they sell clicks to advertisers. This is click arbitrage at its most basic, and something everyone can easily get into.

Let's assume you've got a website about shoes. You spend a couple hours a week on it, blogging about shoes and posting pictures. You decide to do a little paid search advertising and find you can get people to your website at a cost of 10 cents per visitor.

Of course, you don't make any money when someone reads your opinion about sneakers or pumps, which is why you load the site up with advertisements for Nike or Zappos. For this example, let's say you get 60 cents when someone clicks an ad and that a quarter of the people who come to your website click on an advertisement.

So for every 10 cents you spend, you're making 15 cents (25 percent of 60 cents).

Now your job is to do as much marketing as you can at that same return on investment. A million clicks a month turns into $50,000 in pure profit. You don't have to ship anything. You don't have to pay a call center for customer service. You don't have to deal with returns. You don't need to pay rent for a storefront. It goes straight into your bank account.

All these numbers are just examples—you may find it more or less expensive to buy traffic, and the value you sell it for may vary considerably.

The entire click arbitrage model is based on getting clicks for cheap (or free) and selling them to someone else. If you're getting clicks from automated sources that continue to run after you set them up, click arbitrage is like having your own money printing machine. It's what lets many internet millionaires travel the world and get paid while they sleep. It's why I'm writing this chapter on a Tuesday morning from my couch instead of fighting traffic to get to an office downtown.

I mentioned domain parking, but there are a lot of other click arbitrage models that use questionable tactics. There are, however, many click arbitrage business models that are completely aboveboard. I've run several different click arbitrage setups over the years with a lot of success. The best part is that once you put in the work to get everything live, you can more or less walk away while it continues to earn you a steady income.

The easiest way to get started is creating a website about a topic that interests you, or at the very least a topic you don't mind writing about, and sell advertising through an ad exchange like Google AdSense. Before you decide on a topic, though, do some market research.

While topics like cars and credit cards may seem like an obvious place to start, there are plenty of niche

213

topics with advertisers who have very deep pockets. The trick is targeting the phrases and keywords that will let you sell ads for these lucrative offerings.

The experience I got from that job in Georgetown was invaluable. When you spend millions of dollars on advertising, you get a lot of perks, from Pro Bowl tickets in Hawaii to the Google-branded refrigerator that used to sit in the corner of my office. More importantly, you get access and information.

One night, after a steak dinner with a representative of one of the major search engines, I decided to do a little prying.

"What's the most expensive keyword to bid on?" I asked.

The rep thought for a moment. I wasn't sure if he was trying to think of the keyword or if he was wondering whether or not he was allowed to tell me.

"Mesothelioma," he said finally. "We actually had to change our system to allow for higher bids because of that one."

The only thing I knew about "mesothelioma" was from ads on television I'd seen talking about asbestos exposure.

"Lawyers pay big for that one. They put together class-action lawsuits," he said.

The amount a search engine gets paid when a user does a search and clicks on an ad isn't exactly the same as what someone who creates a website full of related content and sells ads would get, but it's in the same ballpark. Advertisers want qualified traffic, and they'll get it just about anywhere they can.

According to what this search engine rep was telling me, anyone with a website about mesothelioma or asbestos that included ads for lawyers was potentially getting hundreds of dollars every time someone clicked on one of those ads.

Simple as that. Somewhere in the world, a reader clicks a button on their mouse, and the website owner is three figures richer.

I'm always interested in finding more ways to generate passive income, so I continued to dig. I asked him if there were any other surprisingly expensive keywords he could share.

"Meth rehab."

That one shocked me as well, until I went home and did a little research. Ultra-luxury treatment centers for drug addiction can charge as much as $80,000 a month. Even the most basic treatment usually costs several thousand dollars. People don't generally ask their friends to recommend a good drug rehab center, so a lot of research is done online to avoid embarrassment.

That's two great niches to start in, but what if you don't want to build a website about aggressive lung cancer or the benefits of going sober?

You don't have to.

There are an infinite number of ways to make money through click arbitrage. You don't even need a traditional website.

One of fastest-growing ways people are making money with click arbitrage is through social media. They build large followings on sites like Instagram, then start posting advertisements for corporate sponsors. Handbags, makeup, watches—social media is like a shopping mall you didn't know you were visiting. Many social influencers are able to skip a pay-per-click model in favor of straight endorsement deals, but it's still the same idea. They're selling clicks and eyeballs.

There are some other ways to make passive income that wouldn't be classified as click arbitrage but also require very little work after the initial setup. Generally these involve selling a nonphysical product. Sometimes it's software, sometimes it's information, but it's usually something that can be easily duplicated on a computer without any additional work, making the cost of goods $0 and the shipping free.

Information products have been a staple for online marketers since the beginning. If you've ever wondered how to do something, chances are there's somebody out there making a living on selling the instructions. There are how-tos on everything from getting the best prices on travel to getting bookings for your indie band.

Some of the more hands-on business models involve coaching. I've even run into quite a few online marketers who have made their fortunes as dating coaches. For a fee, they'll teach you how to be more outgoing in social situations and even optimize your online dating profiles.

Then there are the more questionable "pickup artists." These guys approach a few thousand women, then go to YouTube to post videos of the dozen or so they managed to get phone numbers from. If that doesn't work, they can always hire actresses. The idea is to convince men that they, too, will be able to finally get the women of their dreams by purchasing the pickup artist's program.

I wanted to end this chapter talking about pickup artists because, while many people find the behavior distasteful, applying the same mentality as an entrepreneur is actually a great idea. A recurring theme is the idea that if you approach people of the opposite sex all the time, two things will happen. First, you'll learn what works and what doesn't. Second, you increase your odds of success the more times you try.

In business, you need to keep trying. You need to explore new ideas. Throw things against the wall and see what sticks. "Approach" every idea that comes along - even if you're not feeling up to it or it seems awkward— and you'll increase your odds of success.

Just like in dating, though, don't invest too much until you're sure it's a good idea.

Remember that, unlike a regular job, what you get out of starting an online business is entirely dependent on your skill and how hard you're willing to work. You don't have a boss to impress or a guy down in payroll worrying about how much money you're making. You're 100 percent responsible for your success.

I used to work with a guy whose main goal in life was to make just enough money to quit his job, still be able to pay his bills, and smoke a lot of weed. He managed to do just that by getting free organic traffic from Google to his website and sending it to eBay for a commission. He could have built a big business out of it, but he had everything he wanted and chose to stop working.

I suspect that, like me, you're after a bit more than that. There's a world of clever and shady marketers out there to learn from and endless ways to earn insane amounts of money. Learn to emulate their success, but I strongly suggest you keep your nose clean.

CHAPTER 9

SAVING MONEY & PASSIVE INCOME

"F*&#!!!"

I turned around in my cubicle in time to see the blue armchair flying down the hallway. It crashed into a wall, then bounced for a few more yards until it came to a stop on its side.

"F*&@$#!!"

I slouched down in my chair, trying my hardest to turn invisible. I'd only been at the job for a few weeks, and I was definitely in over my head. Brad, my boss, had a management style I'd never experienced before. I can only describe it as motivation through sheer terror.

I didn't know who was on the receiving end this time, but it sounded worse than anything I'd heard so far, and I wanted to stay out of it. I didn't leave my cubicle for the rest of the afternoon out of fear I'd be stuck by another piece of flying office furniture.

It wasn't until a couple of years later that I finally learned the cause of Brad's massive outburst, and why the armchair had to die.

As the head of the sales department, Brad also oversaw the affiliate program. Just like our company spent tons of money to increase revenue, we had several affiliates who were doing the same. While our company was mostly burning through capital from investment banks, these affiliates were spending their own money to sell our products.

On paper, the affiliates were doing very well, as long as we paid them on time.

Unfortunately, our company had just declared bankruptcy. Despite raising hundreds of millions of dollars, there was nothing left in the bank, and the company owed tens of millions to creditors.

Brad's position meant he was the one who had to call the affiliates and tell them they weren't getting paid. That afternoon, he'd just gotten off the phone with one of our larger affiliate partners. We owed him a lot of money. The affiliate broke down on the phone. He was going to lose his home.

There was nothing Brad could do.

The company's ship was sinking, but thanks to bankruptcy law, a lot of people on the inside had lifeboats. Many other companies were getting stuck with the bill. Our creditors list was a Who's Who of Silicon Valley. Google, Yahoo!, Microsoft, AOL—somehow the company had managed to rack up millions of dollars in debt with each.

Layoffs were looming, and with roughly half the company reporting to Brad, he had a lot of uncomfortable conversations to look forward to.

That one phone call is what finally got to him.

I'll never forget it.

I don't know much about the situation of the guy on the other end of that phone call, but he might have been a dad. I thought of the sheriff coming to my childhood home and knew that, somewhere out there, some other kids might have just been condemned to that same experience.

I've resolved to never let that happen to my children.

LIMIT RISK

Getting wealthy is hard work, but *keeping* wealth can be just as difficult.

Seventy percent of lottery winners are broke within a few years. The skills needed to create wealth are different than the skills needed to keep it, but the work you put into earning money does make you more protective of it.

A lot of people want to be rich because they believe rich people can have everything they want. What they don't realize is that rich people can have *anything* they want, within reason. Not *everything*. There's a big difference.

I'm financially well off. If I really wanted a Lamborghini, I could buy one. What I can't do is buy a Lamborghini, a summer home in New England, a winter home in Miami, a yacht, a private jet, and any other luxury that crosses my mind.

People who've won the lottery or gotten a large inheritance often don't realize this until it's too late.

There's some good news. If you've acquired the discipline to create wealth on your own, you're more likely to develop the discipline needed to hold on to it.

So how do you hold on to it, exactly?

While I support taking bold moves to increase your income, I don't encourage it with money you already have. True, some people have been able to turn millions into billions with risky investments. Maybe you could, too. It's more likely that you'll just lose your millions. That kind of gamble doesn't seem worth it.

After becoming wealthy, I bought a decent house in a good neighborhood and a nice car. I enjoy traveling, which I generally do for work. I don't need eighteen Ferraris in the garage. I don't need a house with rooms I'll never spend time in. I put most of what comes in into "boring" investments.

I like luxuries as much as the next guy, but to me, there's no greater luxury than the peace of mind that comes from not having to worry about money.

DON'T OVEREXTEND

No matter how much of a "sure thing" you believe it to be, never put more into a business venture than you can afford to lose.

If you want to start a business but doing so would require you to put in enough of your money that you'd be financially ruined if things didn't work out, I'd say now is not the time to start that business. Either wait until you have more money or choose a business model that doesn't require so much capital up front.

The chair-throwing incident was still fresh in my mind when I started my own business a couple years later. Like the guy on the phone, I was doing online marketing as an affiliate of another company.

I had to pay for the marketing up front. Eventually I'd get paid for all the commission I earned, but I was on net 30 terms, so if I spent a dollar on marketing, it could be two months before I got it back.

I woke up every morning thinking about the house my family lost when I was a kid. I thought about what would happen if the company I was working with filed for bankruptcy and left me on the hook for two months of marketing spend with no commission income to pay for it.

What I did next wasn't so much business savvy as it was necessity. Using a familiar tactic, I worked as hard as I could to bring in as much business as possible, then every two weeks, I would shut everything down and not spend another dime. I'd turn off every marketing channel I was using and let my web traffic grind to a halt.

It never took long for the phone to ring. The company I was doing work for as an affiliate would call and ask why I wasn't sending any more customers. I'd honestly explain the situation—I couldn't float the kind of money needed to keep tens of thousands of visitors coming to my site every day.

They'd push back, but I wouldn't budge. It's easy to negotiate when you've got nothing left to offer. Eventually they agreed to pay me in full every two weeks, so I never had more than fourteen days' worth of expenses to cover.

I could have gone to the bank and borrowed the money, or I could have gotten more credit cards to cover the marketing expense. It would have been a mountain of unsecured debt, though, and if something happened to the company I was working with, I'd be on the hook for the full amount. For me, that was a nonstarter.

Know what people want. Being a good negotiator is not about having a silver tongue. Sure, it doesn't hurt, but the key to negotiating is fixing circumstances in your favor before you start the process.

If I'd simply called and asked them to pay me every two weeks, they would have said no. Instead, I gave them something they wanted and showed how they'd have to give me something I wanted in return.

I increased my cash flow and limited my liability.

INCORPORATE

Speaking of limited liability, one of the most important things you can do when you start making money is to incorporate. Whether you're starting an online business or buying rental properties, it's the best way to protect yourself and your assets.

I find a limited liability company (LLC) works best for small businesses, but do your research. Every situation is different, and so are the tax and legal implications.

Forming a corporation may sound daunting, but, depending on your state, it can take as little as ten minutes to file the paperwork online. There's also usually a small fee. A few minutes later, you get a confirmation e-mail and you officially own a corporation.

Forming a corporation allows you to legally separate your assets from the assets of the business, which gives you some protection if you get sued down the road or the company goes under. Consult a professional to determine the best corporate structure for your business.

Make sure to pick up business insurance. Depending on your industry, E&O (errors and omissions) insurance might be needed as well.

START BY PAYING OFF DEBTS

Now that you've got money coming in, you might be tempted to start saving it. Don't.

If you've got consumer debt, the first thing you need to work on is retiring it. This type of debt usually has very high interest rates, especially if it's credit card debt. If you're carrying a balance on any of your credit cards, your first investment should be paying it off.

You won't find another investment with a higher guaranteed return than paying off your credit cards.

But my rainy day fund!

You've probably heard over and over that you should have a certain amount of money saved away in case of emergencies. While it's important to have emergency savings, it's still more important to pay off your credit cards. Outside of payday loans, credit card debt is one of the worst ways to shoot yourself in the foot financially.

Let's assume you've got $5,000 in credit card debt, but instead of paying it off, you save up $5,000 for your rainy day fund.

Something terrible happens, and you need to spend the $5,000, emptying your emergency savings. You pat yourself on the back for being prepared. Now you're back to no savings, but your credit card debt has ballooned while you were saving money.

If you'd paid of the credit card, even if you were later forced to put $5,000 back on it, you would have saved yourself from some hefty interest charges in the meantime.

Savings don't generate interest nearly as fast as credit card debt generates more debt.

Not all debt is bad. Some debt can make you wealthier, and that's the kind of debt you want to keep.

Mortgages usually fall under good debt, as long as they're not making you cash poor. If your mortgage rate is 5 percent but your investments are making 10 percent each year, you've got good debt. In other words, if your investments are earning money faster than your secured debt is increasing (say, from mortgage interest), you'll lose money by paying off the debt.

Let's imagine your new business is doing well, and you've managed to save $50,000 that you then invested in the stock market. If you put it in a mutual fund indexed to the S&P 500, the average return each year is around 10 percent.

You get the idea to pay down your mortgage, so you pull your money out of the market and give it to the bank. That's $50,000 less a year that you have to pay interest on. If you've got a 5 percent mortgage rate, that's $2,500 saved each year.

It's also $5,000 of annual stock market returns lost, so unless you're able to successfully time the market and pull out before a steep or prolonged decline, you're actually losing $2,500 a year on average.

Good debt helps you make money.

FINALLY, YOU CAN START SAVING

Remember how I said poor people can't save their way to being rich? Poor people have to spend most of their income on living. Wealthy people have a lot more disposable income that can be put to use creating more wealth.

Saving money and investing it is how you make your money work for you. Compound interest is a powerful tool, and using it to your advantage is the closest thing that exists to a sure bet for your financial future.

To make money work for you, you have to have money. Telling poor people they should save more money to become rich is as ironic as it is insulting. When you're poor, focus on creating additional income. It's easier for someone who doesn't make much to find ways to bring in another $10,000 a year than it is to save another $10,000 a year.

When I was poor, every dollar went to survival. When I started making money, I could pay for all the things I needed, a couple luxuries, and still have enough to build up my savings account.

My income trajectory lifted me into upper middle class just before the 2008 crash. At the time, the common wisdom was still to buy a house worth three to four times your annual income. It didn't matter what your job or cash-flow situation looked like. If you wanted financial security, you had to buy an expensive house.

I bought a house that was equal to my annual income. Everyone said buying the most expensive house you could afford was a sure thing.

There are no sure things. The money didn't seem real. I'd worked hard for it, but I'd been poor so recently it was hard to wrap my head around all the financial freedom I now had. I felt that it could all melt away tomorrow, and, in truth, it still can. Money is easy come, easy go, but the knowledge of how to make money comes hard, and doesn't leave.

When the housing market crashed, I didn't lose much. I had a friend who'd bought multiple properties because real estate was a "sure thing." He declared personal bankruptcy shortly after the crash.

Owning your own home is a decent investment but not a great one. It doesn't produce income and ties up a lot of capital. If you fall on hard times, it's much less stressful to sell off your entire stock portfolio than it is to short sell your home and make your kids pack up their toys.

I'd worked hard for my money, so I wanted to find investments to make my money work hard for me. Instead of buying the biggest house I could afford on my automated income streams, I looked for ways to use the money to create additional passive income.

I enjoy having financial security, and I want to maintain it with as little effort as possible.

The ultimate goal in saving money should be to produce enough passive income to live comfortably. Many people don't hit this point until retirement age. The more money you make, the more money you can invest, and the sooner you'll get to your own "retirement age."

When you build up enough passive income, you don't need to worry about losing your job. If you decide to keep working for someone else, you can feel like your

227

own boss because every day you go to work you're doing it as a choice, on your own terms.

Smart investments are safer than relying on other people for employment your whole life. Anything can happen, but a diversified revenue stream isn't going to walk into the office on a random Monday and announce layoffs.

REAL ESTATE

Your home mortgage can be good debt, provided you don't live in an area where home values are decreasing. A mortgage on a rental property is even better debt. Rental properties are a great way to grow your initial investment while collecting passive income.

Even if you can only rent out a property for enough to cover the mortgage plus basic maintenance ($0 cash flow), your tenants are still paying down your mortgage. After thirty years, you've got a free house.

You want more than that, though.

Unlike most other investments, you can get a relatively cheap loan to buy real estate. It's one of the few options that allow you to walk into a bank and ask them to loan you 80 percent of the investment.

That gives you a lot of leverage. If the bank puts up 80 percent of the money and you buy a house in an area where home values are rising (and continue to rise), for every dollar you invest, you're actually making money off of five dollars. That's leverage.

You pay for that privilege in mortgage interest, but investing in rental properties has been a tried-and-true way to build wealth for millennia.

Let's use a hypothetical $500,000 house as an example. This home is in a high-growth area, and property values are going up by 5 percent a year. If you put 20 percent down ($100,000) and can find renters to cover the mortgage, that $100,000 investment would return $25,000 every year. A 25 percent ROI is fantastic. Of course, not every real estate deal is that lucrative, but there are plenty of opportunities out there.

I was lucky enough to buy a piece of property in a neighborhood where the average house has appreciated almost 10 percent a year for several years.

It cost $900,000 and I put $200,000 down. The interest rate on my mortgage is 4 percent.

If home values continue to rise at the same pace, I'll make 10 percent a year on the $200,000 I invested, and 6 percent a year (10 percent appreciation minus 4 percent mortgage interest) on the other $700,000 that wasn't my money to begin with.

What that works out to is an annual return of 28 percent on my $200,000 investment.

These kind of properties are hard to find, and that number doesn't factor in taxes and other expenses, which are significant. I also know there's very little chance the home value will continue to rise at such an astronomical rate, so I definitely don't expect to make those kind of returns indefinitely—unless I turn it into a rental property.

If you're going to invest in real estate, make sure to find deals where you can at least cover your mortgage costs and expenses with rental income. If you can't find deals like this where you live, look outside of your area. Ideally, not only will tenants pay your mortgage off for you but you'll have some passive income left over each month.

One downside to owning real estate is the property tax you have to pay each year. Most other investments aren't taxed until they're sold, but the government takes a cut from your real estate investments every year you hold onto them. Fortunately, the capital gains you make on the property don't have to be paid until you actually sell it, and you can usually defer those taxes if you use the money to buy another property soon after selling the first.

If it's a home you lived in, you'll likely be able to exclude up to half a million dollars of the sale profit from your taxes ($250,000 if you're single).

Real estate is an investment you can make when you've got money coming in. If you don't have a solid income stream, you probably won't be able to invest in much outside of your own home, if that. Don't look at real estate (or any investment) as a way to get rich quickly. Look at is as a way to turn an existing solid income into a passive money stream.

STOCK MARKET

The stock market is a great tool the middle class can use to get rich slowly. It's much better than sticking your money in a low-interest bank account. For most people, though, stock market investments aren't much different than a savings account—it's a hole they put spare cash into in the hopes that one day they can come back to a large sum of money.

When you're rich, things change. The stock market becomes a source of income. Investing in a relatively safe index fund will typically pay you annual dividends of around 2 to 3 percent of your investment. This is different from the value gained when the price of shares go up. This is money companies pay to their shareholders. You don't have to sell the underlying stock to get paid.

You can hold on to the stocks and let them gain value, while still collecting cash.

Since 2 percent and 3 percent are small numbers, to get a meaningful income, you'd have to invest a considerable amount of money.

A $10,000 investment in dividend stocks can buy you $300 of income a year. That's obviously not enough to live off of. A $10 million investment can get you $300,000 of income. That's enough to live well without ever touching your initial investment, which should also continue to grow.

Since the stock value also goes up over time, selling just enough of your investment to keep a $10 million balance would net you a total average income of a million dollars for doing absolutely nothing.

This is the biggest difference between saving money when you're poor and saving money when you're rich. When you're poor, saving money means you have less to spend on everyday necessities. When you're rich, saving money means extra income to spend on luxuries.

Odds are you're not going to have $10 million to put into a brokerage account in the first couple years after starting your business. Stocks are still a great tool to use. Let compound interest magnify your business profits now that you don't need to use every incoming dollar on necessities.

At some point, you'll be tempted to move away from index funds and start picking individual stocks. The siren call of day trading gets to everyone sooner or later. Do yourself a favor and ignore it.

Passive index funds consistently outperform actively managed funds. Let's assume you're smarter than the guys they have running these multibillion dollar funds, though. The big guys use automation on a scale you can't match. Even if you think you have an edge in smarts, you're going to have to spend a lot of time learning and researching individual companies. It's a full-time job, and you're playing against a stacked deck.

Get all that time back and let the market do what it's supposed to with your money—compound returns. Use the time to find new ways to make money that will feed the compound-return machine.

That said, I do carve out some money for more interesting investments, but nothing that would hurt me if I lost 100 percent of it. It's fun gambling money. If you insist on day trading, take a small portion of your portfolio and use it for active trading for six months. If you beat the odds and outperformed the S&P 500, give yourself more money to play with. If not, find something more productive to do with your time.

I look at the stock market as a multiplier of the money I make elsewhere, not as a way to turn a tiny bit of money into a fortune. Yes, that can happen. You could also win a $200 million Powerball jackpot, but don't count on it.

SELF-SUSTAINING BUSINESSES

If you've built one self-sustaining business that requires very little time and effort to run, there's no reason not to create another one—or two or ten.

Once I've got fulfillment and marketing automated for a business, I'm free to look for the next opportunity to create additional income. The more automated businesses I'm running, the less risk I have financially if something happens to one of them. The more income I make, the faster I can shift my finances to stable, long-term investments. Whether automated or passive, finding ways to increase your income without increasing your workload is the key to unlimited growth.

MOTIVATION

One problem with being wealthy is a loss of motivation. You may have big goals at the start, but it's very easy to slack off once you don't have to worry about paying the rent.

Most people get to a certain point on the wealth ladder and then stop. They've gotten most of what they set out for and don't see the point of continuing ahead for diminishing returns. They grow complacent.

And that's... okay. How wealthy you want to be is up to you.

If your goal is to create just enough passive income so you can live in a trailer and paint or write novels for the rest of your life, good for you. If that's what being wealthy means to you, then you don't have to explain yourself to anyone. Just make sure you've got the automated and passive income in place before you buy the trailer.

CHAPTER 10

WHAT'S HOLDING YOU BACK?

"In any moment of decision, the best thing you can do is the right thing, the next best thing is the wrong thing, and the worst thing you can do is nothing."
—Theodore Roosevelt

PLANS VERSUS ACTIONS

If you're reading this last chapter, it's because you haven't put the book down to go build your empire. Why not?

What's holding you back?

Planning is easy. Action is hard. Chances are it's not a lack of information that's preventing you from starting down the path to financial freedom. If you're like most people, the problem is you have an overabundance of *wanting* but a severe lack of motivation.

Let me start by saying I'm not a proponent of the "law of attraction," "name it and claim it," or any similar ideology that teaches wanting or belief is enough to be successful.

There are people out there who will tell you that if you don't have something, it's because you don't want it enough.

There are a lot of poor people who really want to be rich. Many of them want it more than you do. I spent many years of my life wanting to be rich, but every morning I'd wake up as poor as I was when I went to bed.

Wanting something harder than anyone else won't get you anywhere on its own. All it does is make you more disappointed when you don't get what you want. For practical purposes, wanting is useless.

Wanting has to lead to action.

The way to do that is to turn *wanting* into *motivation*.

We all want to be rich when we're stuck at work or when we get a bill we can't pay. We want to be rich when we see a sports car or drive past a large, beautiful house.

Motivated people remember that feeling hours later when they're at home, sitting on the couch. It drives their actions. Motivation lets an entrepreneur come home from a full-time job and stay up until two a.m. building a business.

BELIEVING

Why do people have a problem turning wanting into motivation? Many people—my younger self included—want to be rich, but we'll let years go by without doing something to make it happen.

I think it's because most of us don't believe it's realistic.

Be honest. When you read about an entrepreneur who struck it rich and sold their company for billions, do you think they just got lucky?

Do you really believe it can happen to you?

Or do you think the system is rigged to keep you down—yet, for some reason randomly lets other people succeed?

That's how I used to think.

While I spent a long time *wanting* to be rich, I didn't believe it was possible. I was making just over minimum wage, and I had no college degree. I had no connections. I had no special skills. It seemed like everyone I went to high school with was so far ahead of me that I'd never catch up.

The only path I saw was to keep working and hope for a 2 or 3 percent raise every year until I found a slightly better job that paid just a tiny bit more than the last one.

I believed there was nothing I could do to improve my situation, so I did nothing to improve my situation.

I got further and further behind. I just didn't know what else to do.

When you don't believe it's possible to get ahead, it's easy for your motivation to revert back to simple wanting.

Again, I'm not saying that believing in something is what makes you successful. Like wanting, it's useless on its own. However, you do need to believe something is possible or you'll never put in the work to make it happen.

I was fortunate enough to get introduced to a world where smart marketers can make their own rules and create wealth without investing a lot of cash. Once I knew it *could* be done, I just had to teach myself how to do it.

DISTRACTIONS

Sometimes it's not about motivation or belief. Sometimes it's distractions that keep us from doing what we know is in our best interest.

It's a lot easier to do something fun now than it is to work on something that might take six months to a year or more to pay off.

Chasing instant gratification can keep you in poverty. Learning how to make money isn't always enjoyable, and the benefits don't come immediately. In the short term, it keeps you from having fun, and our brains don't like that.

Everyone has their favorite distractions.

For some it's drinking and partying. If you're working a tough job, why shouldn't you be able to enjoy yourself on your time off? Many people spend so much time trying to reward themselves for all the hard work they've done that they never take the time to figure out how to reach a point in their lives where they don't have to work so hard.

I admit I've fallen into that practice from time to time. I was lucky, though. I was so poor I usually didn't have enough money to go out and have fun.

Short-term rewards stimulate the emotional part of our brain. It's the same area of the brain responsible for drug addiction. Your brain doesn't get those instant rewards when it comes to improving your life.

In a sense, we're all drug addicts who let short-term rewards hold us back from long-term goals.

Sure, watching TV is not as bad as shooting heroin, but a year's worth of evenings on the couch instead of working toward your goals will do a lot of damage to your prospects.

I'll admit that one of my biggest weaknesses is video games. It's easy to get caught up in low-effort entertainment that constantly rewards the smallest achievements.

It's not just good video games, either. I'm not above wasting time on a mindless phone app, especially if there's a project I'm avoiding. Working on a marketing test that's going to run for a month before there's enough data to make any concrete decisions is boring—beating a game of solitaire and watching the cards fly all over the screen makes you feel like a winner.

Many years ago, I had an epiphany. It was around the time a game called *EVE Online* came out. I was broke, and my prospects looked hopeless. What was the harm in spending my free time playing video games and trying to forget how hopeless my future looked?

Eve Online is a sci-fi game set in space, but what was most unique about it at the time was the player-driven market. Players could form corporations, and the game even had a stock market.

I decided I would figure out how to beat the fake stock market, make a ton of pretend money, and then buy a bunch of pretend stuff.

Before I loaded up the game, I had one of those moments where everything clicks. Why on earth would I want to spend the next six months figuring out how to make money that didn't exist when I could do the exact same thing in the real world and have a bunch of real toys to play with when it was all over?

I'd never be able to fly around asteroids or shoot missiles at space pirates, but buying a plane ticket to Europe whenever I feel like it is a lot more fun.

I realized that money is fun. It's a game. Of course, it doesn't feel like a game when you don't have enough to pay the rent, or when you think making more money means waiting around for your next tiny annual raise. In reality, money is one of the oldest and most exciting games in the world, and the stakes are real.

DO THINGS THAT SCARE YOU

There's another, darker reason why we sometimes let distractions get the better of us.

We're afraid to try.

I know how to watch TV. I know I'm good at it. I didn't know how to build and execute a marketing plan involving paid and earned media.

What if I messed it all up?

That's usually the time I'd reach for the remote. Fear of failing kept me from success for many years, and I wasn't able to escape the cycle of poverty until I overcame it.

Before each major step forward in my financial life, I was terrified. I was scared to ask for a 200 percent raise. I was scared to turn down a job offer that paid double my current salary.

It wasn't easy leaving a low-paying but undemanding job. Too often we stay where we are because we've gotten comfortable and can get through each day with very little effort.

It's important to always be in over your head. When you can tread water, it's time to move on.

STOP BLAMING OTHERS

One last reason many of us don't try is because we believe we're being held back by forces that are out of our control.

It's easier to put the blame on something outside of ourselves. It's a simple way to avoid responsibility.

Stop blaming others.

Stop blaming your parents.

Stop blaming where you started from.

I had nothing. I barely graduated high school and had to move out at eighteen with no money for college. I survived on a fast-food salary. I started with nothing more than the public education they give away for free.

Stop blaming society.

It's not hard because of what you look like, your age, your gender, the color of your skin, where you grew up, or who your parents are. It's hard because it's hard. Nobody is going to give you anything, because then there's less for them. It's true no matter what you look like. You have to earn it.

Don't believe me? Fine—for the sake of argument, let's assume you're right and the world is against you.

So what?

Will you spend the remaining years of your life complaining about how easy everyone else has it, or will you adapt? Are you going to change the world, or are you going to change yourself so you can succeed with the hand you were dealt? Which option do you think is easier?

The best part about modern business is that most of the people you interact with never see your face or hear your voice. What you look like is irrelevant. People see a website, not the owner. I could be an anthropomorphic giraffe, and my customers (and readers) would never know.

DO IT

Now that you're out of excuses, go out and do it. When you put this book down, before you do anything else, come up with a business idea.

You've probably got one idea already that you think can make you money. Maybe it will, maybe it won't.

Here's the secret: there's a good chance it won't. But you should do it anyway.

Your idea doesn't have to be perfect. It doesn't have to be the next Apple or Facebook or Uber. Do everything you can to make it work. Either you'll make money, or you'll gain a better understanding of how to make money.

I've talked to a lot of people who've passed on good business models because somebody else was "doing it already."

That's the best indicator of a good business model. How many grocery stores are there? How many restaurants? If somebody else is already doing it successfully, you know it can work. Get out there and be a competitor.

Maybe it'll work, and you'll steal market share. Maybe it won't. Either way, you'll learn. Don't let the possibility of failure stop you. It's not a possibility. It's a fact of life. Success is when you keep failing until you don't.

So do it already.

HAPPINESS

"Money doesn't buy you happiness, but it buys you a big enough yacht to sail right up to it."
—Johnny Depp, after buying a private island

Go out and build your fortune. I won't tell you how to spend it. Be completely selfish and buy yourself every toy you can think of, or give to others and enjoy changing the world for the better.

It's up to you. Money means choices, and if you've earned the money, you've earned the choices. I want to leave you with this very important truth, though:

Being rich will not make you happy.

Studies have shown that being poor can make you *unhappy*, but once you make enough to be solidly middle class, additional income on its own doesn't add to your happiness.

Money gives you choices, and more opportunities to make the right ones. It gives you both the freedom and the responsibility to pursue your own happiness.

Material things can be fun, and if you can afford them, there's nothing wrong with some frivolous enjoyment. Just know they won't bring lasting happiness.

Experiences and relationships are far more important to leading a happy life.

Just something to think about on that yacht.

101
202

67754948R00146

Made in the USA
Middletown, DE
24 March 2018